Caroline M. Nichols Churchill

Over the Purple Hills

Or, Sketches of Travel in California

Caroline M. Nichols Churchill

Over the Purple Hills
Or, Sketches of Travel in California

ISBN/EAN: 9783337209360

Printed in Europe, USA, Canada, Australia, Japan

Cover: Foto ©Andreas Hilbeck / pixelio.de

More available books at **www.hansebooks.com**

OVER THE

PURPLE HILLS,

OR

SKETCHES OF TRAVEL IN CALIFORNIA,

EMBRACING ALL THE IMPORTANT POINTS USUALLY
VISITED BY TOURISTS.

By CAROLINE M. CHURCHILL,
Author of "Little Sheaves," "Class Legislation," etc.

DENVER:
Mrs. C. M. Churchill, Pub.

1883.

Entered according to Act of Congress, in the year 1876, by
CAROLINE M. CHURCHILL,
In the Office of the Librarian of Congress, at Washington.

TO

MY WESTERN PATRONS,

THIS VOLUME IS RESPECTFULLY DEDICATED

BY

THE AUTHOR.

PREFACE.

I DESIRE to say to the kind and appreciative public that in submitting this edition to their hands without a careful revision, I do so because the labors of the past year have been too great to admit of my using time in that direction. There are many little "corners of speech" which should be worn down and polished, if the only object of the writer were to please the reader with fine language. But as the editions before this have been eagerly bought and read with pleasure by thousands who wish to see California scenery by the aid of a woman's eyes, irrespective of occasional errors, gleefully pointed out by critics so dainty in literary taste that they can neither enjoy anything not perfect, nor find the perfect anywhere—and as there come to the author daily inquiries for the book, even as it is, I feel it a duty to at once give to the world this edition, thereby increasing the store of information in circulation among the world of people, and contributing to their happiness to the extent of this one mite.

THE AUTHOR.

Denver, June, 1884.

CONTENTS.

SAN FRANCISCO AND MAYFIELD	11
MONTE DIABLO	16
BARTLETT'S SPRINGS	25
STOCKTON	39
NAPA	74
LAKE TAHOE	83
CORAL OR ALABASTER CAVE	112
GOING INTO THE YOSEMITE VALLEY	117
WHAT I SAW AND HEARD IN THE VALLEY	135
STRAWBERRYING IN THE YOSEMITE VALLEY	154
VERNAL AND NEVADA FALLS	165
MIRROR LAKE	178
LEAVING YOSEMITE VALLEY	181
VISALIA BRANCH OF CENTRAL PACIFIC RAILWAY	213
MONTEREY	224
VALLEJO	233
PLACERVILLE	239
SALT LAKE CITY	244
THE GOLDEN STATE	253
SAN JOSE IN JUNE	260

FIRST IMPRESSIONS OF A CALIFORNIA EARTHQUAKE	262
SANTA CLARA	265
OVER THE MOUNTAINS TO SANTA CRUZ	267
JUNE WEATHER AND TRADE WINDS	272
SUMMER CLIMATE IN SAN JOSE	277
SAN FRANCISCO	281
THE VERNAL SEASON ON THE PACIFIC COAST	287
THE SAN JOAQUIN RIVER	293
GILROY	298
LOS ANGELES	302
PETALUMA	310
HEALDSBURG	314
SANTA ROSA	317
UPPER PART OF NEVADA COUNTY IN APRIL	318
COLFAX, CAL.	320
GOLD RUN	323
DUTCH FLAT	327
BLUE CANON	330
RENO, NEVADA	333

OVER THE PURPLE HILLS.

SAN FRANCISCO AND MAYFIELD.

LEAVING San Francisco with its damp-freighted winds, I never more fully appreciated the glories of the interior, those portions of the State protected from the unpleasant features of the coast climate. San Francisco cannot be considered an unhealthy city, yet persons with certain constitutional peculiarities and tendencies can never have even passable health upon the west side of the coast range. A family from Detroit, Michigan, were upon the train bound for Monteray, and it was refreshing to hear their comments upon coming from the regions of snow and ice to the plush-covered hills of California. As we near Menlo Park the Detroit people wonder why the forest trees are not cut down and fruit trees planted in their stead. They were answered that the forest trees were preferable, being much cleaner and nicer for the shade of a park. Fruit is so easily raised in this country, and so plentiful, that it is often an incumbrance upon the ground. The trees frequently commence bearing at the age of two and three years, and produce so abundantly as to cause the tree to perish from the draught upon its vitality. My first stopping place is Mayfield. This village is situated in Santa Clara county, surrounded by those beautiful foot-hills which rise like fortifications to encompass the valleys all over the varying surface of this picturesque country. Mayfield is appropriately named; it is as fragrant as a fresh bouquet of flowers, and this vegetable aroma permeates the atmosphere at nearly all seasons of the year. Blessed are the poor who can leave the dingy city and find a chance to subsist in these small towns of the interior.

The land about here is said to be owned in large tracts, so that the small farmer has no chance except by renting; and then it seems difficult to compete with those who do business upon such a gigantic scale. I am in doubt about the number of the population of Mayfield, but they have a corner grocery, a post office, an express office, blacksmith shop, and commodious hotel. In point of size the latter would astonish a stranger not familiar with the demands made upon these interior villages. During summer many of the inhabitants of San Francisco leave the city and search these quiet nooks, where the air is so warm, pure, sweet, and the fragrance of vegetation and stillness make it seem like an earthly paradise. People come in flocks from the coast to get warmed from the chill of damp ocean breezes. It is quite a resort for sportsmen; several alighted with their dogs and guns for a season of shooting. Upon touching the soft green grass the dogs seemed perfectly crazy; they rolled and rubbed themselves in the sweet-scented vegetation and whined with delight. While the men were waiting for a conveyance to take them to the hunting ground, the dogs played scent and hunt around the depot in gleeful anticipation of the game that was to be brought to sorrow. By-and-by the wagons came and they were all tumbled in and commanded to keep quiet. The creatures licked their lips as if to seal them, for it evidently required much effort for them to conceal their enthusiasm.

Mountainview is another station upon the road, the real town or name being located a mile from the depot. The cottages of this little hamlet are exceedingly small and rustic, and the gardens appear like the grounds assigned to precocious youth that the young idea might be trained to agricultural pursuits. Mountainview, like most of these small inland towns, has a good hotel and a picturesque school house, surrounded by the bushy-topped native oak, and the people who support well this public institution are in a fair way to sometime occupy more spacious dwellings and enjoy more extensive gardens. If the human brain is disciplined to think a country must be poor indeed that shall not be made to yield them wealth, but the richest soil and finest climate upon the earth will only produce human animals, (classes excepted,) where the educational interest of the working people is neglected. There is probably no country in the world where people can endure poverty as well as in this. The climate is so mild that with a rude shelter, a few acres of land even rented, two or three goats, or a cow, with ordinary industry, almost any family can gain a subsistence. Many emigrants come here from the older States, recline upon the dignity of American citizenship, refusing to do the work performed by the Chinaman, consequently this enterprising heathen is laying up a competency while the American Micawber is growing rusty and anticipating starvation. Well, it is my opinion that the man who will starve in California, unless by accident, might as well be out of the way. The absurd dignity of extreme poverty can only be equalled by its inconsistency.

April.

MONTE DIABLO.

MONTE DIABLO is the name of a prominence three thousand eight hundred and fifty-eight feet above the level of the sea. This point occurs about twenty-eight miles from San Francisco, and is the terminus of one spur of the coast range. There are many higher points upon the coast than Monte Diablo, but from its peculiar position it gives one of the most extensive landscape views in the known world. The eye has a range from Lasson's Peak in the north to Whitney's in the south, a distance of three hundred and twenty-five miles, giving an area as large as the whole state of New York. The Faralone Islands, forty miles out at sea, can be traced rising in the misty distance like the white walls of a vast storehouse. The checkered streets of San Francisco with its shipping may be seen upon one hand and the dome of the State House at Sacramento upon the other. In the north looms up the weird Buttes and the snow clad Shasta, and in the east the cloud capped Sierras. Thirty-six towns and villages can be counted from this elevation ; bays, rivers and islands lie before the vision as if traced upon a map. Suisun Bay and San Pabloe appear like little inland lakes. It is said that one of the most sublime features of this locality is its storms; as there is neither thunder nor lightning accompaning them, there is little to fear except the temporary effect of the wind. The voice of the storm is an indescribable high toned roar, the crash, din and tumult being really enjoyable. These coast mountains have not the grand old pine forests of the Sierra Nevadas, the growth being limited to scrub oak and small shrubs and many of them only the dried grasses to cover the naked earth. Still there is something attractive about them if it is only to give a crooked variety of outline to the horizon. The foot-hills are fertile and susceptible of cultivation as well as making an excellent range for grazing purposes. I tarried four days about Monte Diablo, and had the pleasure of seeing one of the most gorgeous sunsets that I ever beheld.

The ocean fog and mist came flying up the ravine past the hotel in such distinct vapory forms as to cause one to speak of them as living creatures. In fact the cañon seemed a thoroughfare where the fog was drafted by the air from the ocean and valley to certain points near the mountain tops. The course of these flying vapors was so marked, and they flitted so steadily but silently by that they formed a feature of great interest. The doors of the hotel had been closed to prevent any straggling damps from entering; everything appeared foggy and gloomy. All at once a west window was lighted up, as if by the sudden blaze of a bonfire. A young girl screamed and looked frightened, exclaiming "O dear, the valley is all on fire!" As the sun was sinking in the west and his beams assumed the right focus, all this gloom changed in the twinkling of an eye, and the fog became a bright flame color, still keeping its billowy identity. Viewing it from the elevation of the hotel some distance above the valley the effect was wonderful. In a few moments it changed from a flame color to a light yellow, and as the sun disappeared it shed a beautiful pink shade upon the mist, giving the ravine and whole valley the appearance of being draped in undulating folds of pink tarlton. This gradually faded to white, then to a leaden blue, and the last that I saw of the scene, those misty ghosts were chasing one another up the ravine, just as they did before the illumination, only a little faster and with vapors more condensed.

The next morning I ascended the summit that I might see what had become of those foggy flocks driving for the hill tops the night before. There they were to my astonishment, having reached a certain altitude they had halted to rest, hovering over the foot-hills upon the south side of Monte Diablo, completely covering them from sight, like so many snowy fleeces, for they had changed the lead colored traveling dress and were all robed in white. The summit of Diablo was entirely above this ocean of mist and upon the north the landscape was as clear as if the hills upon the south side of the point were not entirely enveloped in this downy covering. What a kind provision of nature! the drafts of air just suck these clouds of fog up the ravines; here they cling around the hill tops until eaten up by a tropical sun, or are poured out in draughts of rain, which runs into the valleys, giving this water first to the mountains, next to the valleys, lastly the rivers. Truly,

"He moves in a mysterious way,
His wonders to perform."

At this season of the year the clouds do not amount to rain, although they moisten vegetation wherever they appear, that is all along the coast and save the necessity of irrigation.

Old Sol in his morning rounds searches out every obscure hollow or indentation where vapors have dared to gather during his temporary absence, and when his beams strike the spot little spirits of vapor are seen to rise up as distinctly and rapidly as the smoke from the flue of a chimney and are gone in a moment, swallowed by this yellow-faced ogre. Looking down upon this ocean of fog, I could imagine it peopled with ethereal beings, as it would require but an occasional flap of angel wings to keep afloat upon this beautiful sea of glory.

When sinking nearly through, one could obtain a rare view of the scarlet poppy fields, the soft green hills and picturesque animal life peacefully grazing, and while the sun is scattering the fog-cloud, I look to the north and see the discolored waters of the Sacremento and the San Joaquin rivers with their soiled tributaries slowly coursing along, uniting in one body before passing the Golden Gate to enter the great peaceful ocean. Tracing these rivers from their source until they reach their destiny, how much they resemble the course of human life. Falling from the clouds a pure snow-flake, pillowed for a time upon the lofty mountain tops, there to be warmed into liquid bodies, carried below by circumstances to the great world of usefulness, for a time maintaining its purity of color to the admiration of the sentimental tourist and practical native, dispensing blessings to thirsty vegatable and animal life. As it descends further, it is concentrated into iron pipes and wooden flumes and dashed with Niagara force into the red clay bank to start from its hiding place the yellow gold dust which it baptises to a new life of usefulness. Here the die is cast, henceforth until the sea is reached, must the river which first came to earth a snow-flake, travel through all its life of utility with the stain of soil upon its bosom, and the signs of its uses marked in all its varying phases. The days of its romance are ended, the dashing cascade and coquetish waterfall, its wayward wanderings through groves and woods, its deep and quiet thoughtful moods, its spreading out to hold the plain then shrinking to its banks again, an emblem of our life to lend, it chafes its banks until the end.

If it were not for contemplating the destruction of life and property in the valleys, the rising of those rivers from Monte Diablo would be one of the grandest sights in the world. Swollen five times their natural size, filled with monster trees and drift-wood of every conceivable shape, the mountain sending their furious little torrent down their sides, and the roaring rapid current lending the facination of force to the scene, all together forming a fearful, moving picture, while we could stand on Monte Diablo's top and view the landscape o'er. These scenes have the effect upon my nature to arouse sleeping sublimity and veneration, and once a day I resolve myself into a methodist prayer meeting, stealing away around the hills where I have a fine view of the valley, here to sing sacred pieces and read a selection from the Psalms of David. I found peculiar comfort in reading aloud the Church of England burial service, for I imagine the green, oblong mounds to be the graves of the gods where they have lain down to rest themselves after some very fatiguing labors, with their heads reclining heavenwards, and have forgotten to rise again and become a part of the everlasting hills to share alike in their misty cloud-caps, purple mantles and beautiful dresses of green and autumn brown. The birds seem to catch the inspiration of the scene and remain suspended on fluttering wing, hovering over the enchanted valley.

I returned to the Central Pacific Railroad and

practical life by the Sanramoon Valley to Livermore. This route to Monte Diablo is most desirable. The Sanramoon Valley is one of the most productive spots in the whole State and is under fine cultivation. Fields of wheat were standing fence high, green as a meadow, and level as a house floor, and so heavily laden as to tremble in the breeze from their weight. Orchards loaded with fruit, in fact, everything wearing a look of luxurient prosperity. The soil is dark and rich. Shade trees are planted for miles along the public highway. The meadow lark, and linnet, quail and robin, all were singing " more wheat, big wheat, sweet wheat, we'll eat the wheat."

May.

BARTLETT'S SPRINGS.

FROM Cloverdale, which is the present terminus of the Northern Pacific Railroad, the route to Bartlett's Springs is literally upward and onward. After reaching the Springs one fully realizes that they lie over the hills and far away. The ride of twenty-seven miles from Cloverdale to Kelserville is about the same in points of interest as the mountain roads usually are throughout the State. The scenery grand, ever varying, and every change bringing with it new beauties in the singular formation of the mountain landscape. There is the finest variety of wild flowers upon this route that I have ever observed upon any of the mountain roads in California. Leaving Cloverdale at six A. M., we arrive at a little place called Kelserville at two

p. m. Here again is verified the adages which declare that "there is *nothing* in a name," "and that a rose would smell as sweet by any other." The tourist will readily concede that as a village Kelserville comes as near to nothing as anything can, and at the same time have been duly christened; also that it would smell as sweet by any other cognomen. There are several gas springs located about one-half mile from the hotel. These openings emit the most abominable gaseous odors that are manufactured in his Satanic majesty's kingdom. An iron tube is placed in one of these infernal outlets, which collects the gas in a stream, so that when ignited a beautiful blue blaze shoots up about two feet in height. This matter, which a moment before belonged to the invisible world, now becomes a living reality to more than one of the senses. These springs must be visited at night, as the color of the burning gas is so pale at daylight as to be scarcely visible. The practical mind at once feels a longing to utilize this liberal production of mother nature, and the imagination sets to running pipes miles away over the hills, to carry this illuminating fluid to towns and cities, where it may be used for lighting streets and dwellings, for chemical and scientific purposes, and the convenience of the culinary department, and thereby fulfill the destiny of nature to supply the wants of the primitive God-Man. The mind of the visionary religionist creates an altar where sacrifice could be offered to the Maker of the universe, and where the fires of eternal incense might ascend upward forever.

How consistent! to make an offering to the God of the religionist of the most abominable chemical production of his Satanic majesty's infernal laboratory.

Leaving this part of the kingdom inferno, we proceed seven miles through a small tillable vale of land to the village of Lakeport, situated upon the margin of Clear Lake. The county was called Lake because of the numerous bodies of water coming to the surface, as if to fill the mouths of extinct craters. The town of Lakeport contains about two or three hundred inhabitants, is the county seat, has a new brick courthouse, and a row of beautiful native oaks standing in the center of the streets. I think there are as many as thirty of these mighty shades along in one row, spreading their sheltering arms impartially over all who pass upon the street, as if bestowing a blessed benediction. Clear Lake is a body of water so exactly in appearance and surroundings like Washoe Lake, in the State of Nevada, that one feels as if viewing the same little American Galilee. A small steamer is in course of construction for navigating this lake. This body of water, which appears to the beholder to be about three miles in length, is in reality thirty-six miles, but winds its way through the valleys and gorges of the mountains, so that it is ever reappearing when one is miles upon the road, like a beautiful face seen again after a supposed final parting. This country is very mountainous, with a remarkably fine climate, and is settled mostly with invalids. They are far from market, with surroundings so rugged as scarcely to be accessible to railroads. The consequence is the inhabitants feel poor, and talk as if hopelessly resigned to this condition of things. I do not believe that it need be true of Lake county that it shall never develop wealth because of not being an agricultural district. When its resources for rearing sheep, goats and cattle are fully known, we shall see that wealth can be produced from something besides wheat.

In this route to Bartlett's the road takes a winding ascent over the mountains. As we pass we discover campers all through these hills, who have come to recreate for a time in the delightful mountain atmosphere. In a climate of such equality of temperature it seems absolutely necessary for its inhabitants to have a change of altitude, in order to secure the atmospheric elements supplied in other countries by the greater variation of the seasons. It is surprising what an amount of physical exercise and fatigue one can endure when in a mountain climate, if the altitude is not too great. And how one will sleep! and sleep seems so refreshing. To me the mountains are earth's paradise. I would rather be a herder of sheep or cattle in this pure breath of nature's than live in a palace within the foul scented city, with its endless bustle and everlasting crash and din of commingling noises. It is no longer a wonder to me that these mountaineers cleave to their native hills until they become like wild men, in many respects closely resembling the flocks they attend. Many of them permit their locks to become an entangled mass, as inaccessible to comb or brush as the impenetrable shrubs of their own hills. How delightful from a pulpit of rocks to declaim one's best productions to the wondering sheep and goats, and pour out sweet-strained music, to be encored by the ever appreciating echo of the surrounding hills. To descend with a sense of having discharged a duty to the *masses*, (of rock) and receive the congratulatory paw of one's faithful assistant, Bowser, who is clothed (if not for this occasion especially) in silken coat, with handsome fringe running from the tips of his beautiful ears to the point of his toes; then I am sure of the love of an humble, faithful friend in one of God's creatures at least. I expect much of humanity; and because they fall so miserably short of these expectations I am inclined to feel for them contempt, and to seek companionship in the lower order of creatures, who, if they are not intellectual equals, do not manifest the disagreeable traits of the inferior human animal.

Bartlett's Springs are situated in the northern part of Lake county, upon a spur of the coast range. They are about forty miles east from Ukia and sixty from Colusa. Any one desirous of knowing the locality can easily find it by referring to the map of California containing the counties or the county seat towns. There are no settlements to speak of within twenty-five or thirty miles of this location, although stores and saloons may be found hidden away in some silent ravine, where excursionists, campers and stragglers can procure almost any common staple, from whisky and tobacco to bag strings, paper collars and patent medicines. These springs were discovered to possess medicinal properties by the owner of the land, a mountaineer, by the name of Bartlett, who knowing the water to be sweet, pure and cold, came here when sick, as he supposed unto death, and camped near them, expecting to lay his bones here, and that, too, in a brief time. This water he used for cooking, drinking and washing. The results were that in a few days he began to improve, his rheumatism left him entirely, and he became perfectly sound. This discovery was made in 1869. Since then many have sought and found relief in using these waters. The man, Bartlett, is said to be from one of the Southwestern States, is a person of excellent common sense, but with no other education than that acquired by the wild hunter and sheep herder in pursuit of a most primitive livelihood. Entirely unaccustomed to the associations of the wealthy or educated, he has very naturally formed strong prejudices against classes of human beings of whom he knows nothing scarcely, hence he utterly refuses to let this property pass into the hands of the capitalist who could make it one of the most desirable places of resort upon this coast. The property has been leased for a term of three or four years. For this length of time it will not pay the lessee to expend anything for permanent improvements, so that the buildings that are put upon the place are of the most unsubstantial character, being built mostly of red wood shakes. There are about seventy-five of these structures upon a piece of table land where the springs come forth. Some of these cabins are accommodated with a chimney running up on the outside after the manner of the chimneys in Southern States, and many families prefer to do their own cooking. The hotel is a long wooden structure, mostly dining room and porch, there being little room for lodgings, most of the boarders at the hotel lodge in the shake cottages. Myself and lady friend were shown to one of these cabins measuring eighteen by twenty, divided into four compartments, and facetiously called the "Cliff House." We were soon installed in one of these quarter sections at ten dollars a head per week, board included. When our trunks were placed inside there was only room enough for one chair, so it became necessary when both were at home for one to always be in a reclining position, as the bed was so high as to preclude the possibility of using it for a sofa. Our visitors were received upon the outside of the house where two persons could be seated at once upon a discarded apple box turned up side-wise. The bedsteads were of the most simple possible structure, so loosely put together as to tremble and totter with the weight of one person; they were clear from bugs, thank fortune, and I never slept better than when at these Springs. We found the hotel table very well supplied with edibles, only in a few articles did the parsimony or small economy of the proprietor manifest itself. The potatoes were so exceedingly minute as to really provoke mirth whenever they were presented. At last I ventured to ask where in the world or in California were those potatoes raised. He answered very meekly that they came from Colusa, a poor place for potatoes. This satisfied me for the time, as then I had never been in Colusa. I afterwards spent two weeks in that town, and am inclined to believe the above statement a slander on Colusa, as I saw no insignificance in anything raised in those parts.

I think now that those vegetables were imported; not a native of California at all. The milk was excellent; indeed it might have been watered from Bartlett's spring without injury to the flavor, as this water is nearly as sweet as maple sap. The water known as Bartlett's spring, boils up right at the foot of one of those stupenduous land bubbles which form these mountain ranges. It is clear as crystal, and too cold to take into the system until its temperature is modified by standing awhile after being taken from the spring. There is not a speck of anything to be seen in this water, neither animate or inanimate. It has a sweetish taste, as if there might be an ounce of the best loaf sugar to three gallons of water. This is supposed to be arsenic. I did not see the report of a chemical analysis, although I understand there has been one made, but not entirely satisfactory to the chemist himself. The most wonderful characteristic of this water is that it will not corrode metals. Tin is brightened by being brought in contact with this fluid, and iron lying in its outlet will not rust. Metals are made brighter by being infused in its waters.

There is another spring known as the Bartlett Soda, lying a short distance from *the* spring; this is strongly impregnated with iron, and every thing about it is colored with this sediment.

The water produces the same stinging sensation made by drinking the manufactured soda. Near this spring is a huge, brown bowlder, standing out as if desirous of plunging into the table land lying below, and only prevented by some invisible outside pressure. This rock has a history, which I will relate as told me by a resident of the place ever since the springs were discovered. An insane man of the harmless order of lunatics was brought here to test the healing waters upon the diseased brain. One day he was taken with a violent desire to commit suicide ; before preventive measures could be brought to bear, he had climbed to the top of this rock and taken a Sam Patch leap into the ravine below. He fell upon the mansineta and aside from a few scratches sustained no physical injury — scrambled out of the brush, and arrived at the hotel, a distance of a couple of hundred yards, a perfectly sane man, and has had no return of the symptoms of insanity since ; and this occurred three years ago.

At the time I visited Bartlett's, about two hundred and fifty persons were upon the ground, mostly persons in moderate circumstances who had come to be benefitted by the healing waters. The spring is covered by a small rough building, with two or three rude benches on the outside. Here twenty or thirty men may be seen sitting at all times of the day ; poor, forlorn, miserable looking creatures ; many of them victims of bad whisky, and its general train of results ; tottering and feeble in health, tattered in raiment, and shattered in hopes and fortune. Many of them are benefitted by these waters, and many a pallid face seen here can only be benefitted by the waters of eternal oblivion. Poor humanity, how I wish it had entered into the plan of divine economy to have made man with as much judgment about taking care of himself as the beasts seem to possess. These men linger hopefully near this spring, because in most instances too weak to walk three times a day back and forth from their cabins. They prefer the water fresh, but I am convinced that it is not as well taken into the stomach too cold. The efforts of this group to keep in the shade of the spring house, reminded me of the story of Rip Van Winkle, whom it is said crawled around a shade tree with such **lazy** precision that the time of day could be determined by his attitude as accurately as by a sun dial.

This is the class of sufferers who appeal to the sympathies of the original discoverer, and make him anxious to keep the place from those who would convert it into a fashionable resort. Some persons come and stay three or four months, while the hapless pleasure seeker, pampered with luxuries and entertained with amusements at home, generally leave at the end of two days, declaring emphatically that Bartlett's Springs have no charms for him. There is not a thing in the way of amusements, unless it be one billiard table, and one poor suffering violin, brought here for treatment likely. There is not a swing, a croquet set, nor piano, nor shaded platform for dancing, speaking or concerts. There is, however, in course of erection, a house to be used for such purposes, and it was with much discretion and forethought placed at a proper distance from the camp, so that the sick should not be disturbed with the sounds of revelry. This place is wonderfully silent. People with little surplus vitality have no strength to spend in making a noise. The wheels of business move slowly about — there seems less need of work or bustle when people are languishing between life and death, or waiting for the worn physical system to recuperate.

I spent the fourth of July, 1874, in this place, and never since in the United States, did I enjoy the Nation's birthday as well.

> Not a drum was heard, not a shouting note,
> Not a gun was fired from hill or moat,
> Not a cracker burned, not a rocket fizzled,
> Not a house was fired, not an engine whistled ;
> But thoughtlessly, carelessly, every one stirred,
> As if the birth of the Nation had never occurred

Ailing horses are frequently brought to these springs and are said to be benefitted the same as the human family. One little dog and his (*faithful*) master attracted considerable attention as they trudged past three times a day to visit the healing spring. The dog is a little blue, Scotch terrier, and came to this bustling world in 1852, is consequently twenty-four years of age, about forty years younger than his kind and appreciative master, in whose interests and love he has always shared, and who are now grown old together. This man is a well-to-do old bachelor, a native of the Southwestern States, with limited education, but possessing much native shrewdness and a brave, kind heart. This canine has been his constant companion for years and been the recipient of the love and tenderness most men bestow upon their wives and little ones. He comes to this spring every summer with the understanding that his own health is perfect, but that Pinto's appetite is poor, and that he is in need of a change. One of the peculiar features of interest about this camp, is to contemplate the pile of wooden staves laid aside from the influence of this wonderful spring upon rheumatic invalids. When the thermometer rises to ninety-five or a hundred, the heat becomes almost unbearable in our little cribs of cabins, which are too transparent to form much of a protection from the merciless rays of the scorching sun. The ground upon which the cabins are located forms a kind of basin surrounded on all sides by hills which reflect the rays of heat, and when it is airy and comfortable upon these elevations, the heat upon the table land will be intense. Boughs were brought and placed upon the top of the "Cliff House," and a little porch made and covered with green branches, and then it became necessary to hang up our blankets in front of the porch in order to screen our eyes from the glaring light and heat which fell with such intensity upon the yellow sand.

I came to the springs because afflicted with a peculiar form of indigestion, having a sensation after eating as if the stomach had been filled with a dry, hard substance, like gravel. This sensation would continue sometimes two hours, then disappear and the appetite be as good as ever for the next meal. Writing or study aggravated these symptoms very much, and taking fluids into the stomach seemed to make it worse. The first experiment I tried was to wait until the sensation was fully established after eating, then I drank a pint of this water cold as it came from the spring. In a few minutes that sense of dryness had left the gastronomic department, and never returned during the nine days which I sojourned at the springs. When I left I took a jug of the water with me, and had no return of these symptoms while this lasted. When it was exhausted, I had to wait three days for another supply to reach me, and those symptoms returned; upon using the water, they again disappeared. I will here say, if I had taken a like quantity of any other fluid after eating, it would have arrested the process of digestion and caused vomiting. This water acts as a gentle purgative upon the bowels; seemed to quiet the nerves and produce a desire for sleep. I took a sound nap of an hour every alternate day, and that seemed to make no difference with a refreshing, dreamless sleep of eight hours at night.

LEAVING BARTLETT'S SPRINGS FOR COLUSA.

At six o'clock A. M. July 12th, all was in readiness for a start, our load inside the coach being composed entirely of feminines of the following order: Myself and lady friend, two young ladies and two little misses. Was there ever such a number of pairs accidently brought together before? Two masculines were seated upon the outside, one as driver and the other as assistant. We were drawn by a team of four large mules, one unaccustomed to harness, and represented by the driver as a little wild. The road is new, narrow and very rough. This, with the fractious addition to our locomotion, inspired the whole party with a sense of insecurity anything but pleasant. The coach tore away through a combination of manzanita, chaparral, greasewood, sage-brush and the bush of a thousand thorns, occasionally bumping us over a hard-head. This had the strange effect upon one of the party to cause her to relate the old story of Horace Greeley and Hank Monk. We had not gone more than two miles, but I had in that time learned too much of physical suffering to raise a voice against this mental affliction, consequently bore it without a smile. When passing into a valley we were met by a couple of strangers, Missourians I should think, dressed in cure colored unmentionables, one carrying in his hand a canvas-covered ham, the other carrying a sack of edibles upon his shoulder. These men caught sight of our party inside, and looked with unshrinking gaze until the coach came opposite, and then they stood stark still and stared until the driver stopped the coach and said, "Gentlemen, do you want anything?" They never averted this gaze to see the source of the questioning, but answered with a drawling "N-o-o," as if in a study of too profound a nature to be disturbed with idle interrogations. The little girls tittered, the young ladies giggled, the matrons smiled, the assisting man grinned, and the driver "haw-hawed" right out. The man ahead informed us that they continued to gaze in wonder and astonishment until the coach was out of sight. "Well, did I ever!" was the generally expressed sentiment, and the circumstance was soon forgotten. It is a little singular, considering how many robberies are committed upon this coast, that not one of our party screamed or thought of fainting. We did not have Wells & Fargo's box nor Uncle Sam's mail; only a load of females, a cargo often coveted, but seldom surreptitiously appropriated.

Shortly after passing these wondering strangers, we came to pass a couple of gentlemen riding in a one-horse buggy, drawn by a beautiful bay. Two handsome shepherd dogs followed on foot. This mountain road only provides half passes, and this party met our mule team where there was not even a half pass. The mules were driven into the bank, until, as if in anticipation of coming events, they placed their ears close to their heads. The beautiful bay was reined out, and from the unevenness of the ground, fell floundering in the brush. The gentlemen in the buggy looked serene, as if perfectly confident of the success of mind over matter, finally concluded to descend and disentangle as far as possible. A word of encouragement to the patient horse, and he lay perfectly quiet while the buggy was tilted up by hand and passed by our formidable hubs. Then the harness was loosed and the horse commanded to rise, which he did with the caution of a reasoning being. When once fairly on his feet, in the road again, was patted and praised for this exhibition of good sense, a method of treatment that horses well know how to appreciate. The two handsome dogs were on hand, lolling out their red tongues, appearing as much interested as any one of the party. In the meantime our mules danced and kept their ears in position for anything that might occur till the cracking of the brush ceased. I became so much interested in the extrication of the horse, the prancing of our own team, and the two dogs, that I found myself outside of the coach standing upon the side-hill where the brush was so compact that I could not have walked a rod if a grizzly bear had been in prospect. I wonder why drivers will always be so profuse in their advice to nervous women at such times, declaring, with vehemence, that there is no danger. I belong to a class of women who have not unlimited confidence in the assertions of man at any time. Providing there is no danger, women frequently suffer more from fear and nervousness than they would, perhaps, if the danger was realized, and where is the economy in endeavoring to compel forbearance when the trouble of alighting will quiet all fears. After his passing event, we are again on our crooked and narrow way. Presently the driver calls the attention of the party to a deer walking leisurly along. The mules prepare their ears; the children shout in surprise at the creature's indifference. One of the men express a desire for a gun, while I enjoy the fact that he is not to be slain, as there is not the remotest chance for me to get a piece of his delicious carcass. Teams now frequently pass us upon the table lands; knowing the hour that the stage is expected, take this precaution in order to avoid the above mentioned scene. It is a wonder to me that there are not laws enacted compelling every teamster to put bells upon his horses or mules while driving over these fearful mountain roads. The turn-outs seen in this remote region are so covered with dust that it is quite impossible to distinguish color. They prove to be mostly of the semi-civilized race, who emigrate from Missouri and Texas, wear the tan-colored unmentionables, and in many instances pride themselves upon their virtue, being too ignorant to sin. These people are in just the right stage of barbarism to accept the Catholic religion, and are surely better prepared for a patriarchial or monarchial form of government than to make laws for themselves in a republic. The Southern and Southwestern States are going over to the Catholic church in a body, with the understanding that Catholicism will some day overthrow this government. To the thinker this does not seem like very effective policy, inasmuch as the Protestant educates the brain of the masses, while Catholicism keeps the masses uneducated as far as in them lies, consequently the Protestant stands the chance of ruling over the Catholic even at a disadvantage in numbers. How queer it would seem to think of the French, Italians, Spanish, or Irish, as rulers over England, Scotland, Germany, or any of the Protestant races. Just here I will say that no race of people where the masses live on such food as "hog and hominy," can ever compete with those who have more range in diet. From what I am able to observe, I should think that a limited monotonous diet would cramp the calibre. Even the fairly educated among these people do not seem to possess the power of reasoning to any great extent, but are controlled by prejudices that would hardly be excusable in barbarians. Nations, let them be republican, or what they may, are culpable for the ignorance of their people, and must take their punishment for such neglect in crime, disrespect, prejudice, and rebellion. How can a man have any respect for the institutions of a country where he has been permitted to grow up in such groveling ignorance as to be incapable of comprehending a single advantage of its institutions over those of others? If the law of Christianity which commands man to love his neighbor as himself, had been observed or carried out consistently, the money sent to christianize the heathen in foreign lands, would have been given to the southern portion of our own country to educate the "poor white trash." These people have moved westward, ignorant as barbarians, and more prolific, and are raising up a generation of vipers little in advance, if any, of the native Mexican. The border ruffian, with others of that class of bloodletters, had mothers who took the same position in the family as the native Australian women or the wife of a North American Indian does, living in the most primitive manner, performing the drudgery of the household without the advantages of civilization. Those that we meet are mostly performing pilgrimages to the springs for the purpose of regaining lost health. The shadowy teams, rickety wagons, loaded with household plunder, the scrawny women and numerous progeny, bring to mind the childish riddle of Saint Ives — As I was going to Saint Ives I met seven wives; each wife had seven sacks; each sack had seven cats; each cat had seven kits—kits, cats, sacks and wives, how many were going to Saint Ives? I am not prepared to state whether the foregoing can be classed with conundrums, whether it is an example in mental arithmetic, an algebraic problem, or, in the language of our Anglo Saxon grandmothers, if it is a riddle; will leave the reader to decide. The road gets smoother as we progress, because it comes within the range of more travel. The mountain breeze is delightfully cool and fragrant from the perfume of vegetation. One variety of tree has shed its leaves in a mass; they seem to have all fallen at once, and lie perfectly undisturbed by the passing zephyr, enjoying their faded glory; being exactly the color of straw. I thought at first sight that the straggling camper had emptied the contents of his primitive bed upon the hill-side, but upon closer observation it proved to be the leaves of a particular tree. The spreading oak is just putting out a new crop of leaves while the old ones are still fresh in their original beauty, giving this magnificent tree, a variety of shade from the pea-green to the darkest color of the oak leaf. The same tree in this country adapts itself to the climate, performing the office of regeneration in an entire different manner from what it does in a northern latitude. The team labors slowly up the mountain, descending with more rapidity, hence making about the same number of miles in the same length of time as they would providing they were upon the level. As we approach the plains of Colusa county a hot breeze occasionally passes over us. Some of our party venture the opinion that this simoon is maunfactured upon a barren spur of the coast range lying between us and the great plains. These hills do appear perfectly terrible with their bare brown sides under a scorching July sun. We are informed that this heated breath comes from the plains beyond; that it is not the province of mountains to manufacture hot winds, as their very altitude makes that an impossibility. At the foot-hills large flocks of sheep are to be seen huddling together beneath the scanty shade of the now scattering trees. Poor things, how they must suffer from the heat of the scorching sun. The winds may be tempered to the shorn lamb, but the burning rays of old Sol never. The shepherds who attend these flocks are themselves a peculiar "institution," for a general thing showing less sense in their domestic concerns than that manifested by the field mouse. The people are not the owners of the flocks, only hired to do the work of taking care of the sheep that cannot be well entrusted to a dog. Their huts are built between the hills, upon the hot sand, without the grateful shade of a single twig. Of course these houses are only inhabited during the night, or sleeping hours, so that it does not make so much difference. It is likely if there is a shade tree anywhere near the shepherd will have the benefit of it. I have learned that it will not do to draw comparisons rashly, or to put too severe a sentence upon the modes of life adopted by those occupying widely different places in the plan of the universe. If a good housewife were at this moment to sit in judgment, or pass sentence upon the appearance of my room and wardrobe, it would take a great deal of explanation to correct the prejudices that might arise in the mind of a well regulated person who had never drawn upon her innocent imagination for the result of four years steady travel upon one's wardrobe and methodism in general. To one not acquainted with the peculiarities of this dry climate, it does not seem possible for sheep or goats to exist upon these apparently verdureless hills; still we are informed that this is excellent pasturage. Hence the presence of these numerous flocks which are often driven miles to reach food when they have exhausted any particular locality. In this seasonless climate the curing process is complete, the moisture of the winter rains being sufficient for a perfect growth of vegetation. The grasses stand upon the ground perfectly ripe and dry, containing all their original juices, having had no rains or dews to bleach them of their virtues.

We now reach Colusa county plains. This area of land, fifty miles wide and two hundred miles long, is a dead level, and has the appearance of having been the bed of a lake or sea. This vast plain is converted almost entirely into wheat farms. Thousands of acres of bright stubble stands bristling in the glowing sun, for the wheat is all cut by the tenth of July. The numerous stacks seen in the distance suggest the idea of many villages composed of thatched buildings, and the mirage comes to make the illusion more complete, and many of the stacks are represented double, standing bottom upwards, or rather hanging top downwards. It is very strange how a little patch of sandy land, with a few weeds growing near, will look, with the help of mirage, exactly like a lake of water, with trees growing upon the margin, and one can see the shadows as plain as anything. Colusa county may well be called "the old bachelor's paradise."

The dingy little cribs in which they live, without shade of tree, or other comfort, where there should be spacious farm houses, show clearly the absence of the refining influence of woman. And the fact that these farmers may be frequently seen studying navigation at the neighboring tap rooms is another evidence of a want of the vigilance of woman, who, if she were here, could local-optionize the place and protect man, as he will not protect himself, from his manifold infirmities. Occasionally a sluggish stream finds its way across this level plain. Little birds, that appear to be lost, sit panting with uplifted wing, apparently without life to fly and seek a shade in the woods which are miles away. When we are so far at land upon this plain as to be out of sight of every thing except stacks and stubble, a scene presents itself as startling as it is novel. The road ran by a sink-hole, or a tunnel in the ground, about twenty feet across. This curious well was filled with muddy-looking water. Upon approaching it, ten or a dozen human heads are seen bobbing up and down upon its surface, in motion as if trying to dodge a missile. As one wonders in attending a meeting in the country where all the people can come from, so I exclaimed, "Where on earth, or upon this plain, did those men come from?" The farm houses are so small as to have escaped our memory, if they did not escape our vision. Our informant, the man ahead, says that these are farm hands who come here to bathe, as those little cribs of houses do not afford very extensive accommodations for its tenants; that every one of those smiling faces have a live body buried in the depths of this isolated well. This was indeed a rare sight — an oasis in the desert of stubble, without a tree or shrub to mark its whereabouts. There are tracts of alkaline lands upon this plain, that are useless for farming, and because of the long dry season, the dust becomes so dense upon the roads that the houses are built mostly as long way as possible from the main road and reached by lanes. This, and the houses being so small, gives the country the appearance of being under cultivation without the corresponding improvements. Another drawback to the country is the fact that the land is owned in very large tracts, being worked by tenants, men who have no families, and consequently not permanent, while the real owner, like the sheep owner, is living with his family comfortably in some town or village, perhaps city. All countries develop peculiar features to themselves because of the difference of the soil and climate. The real farm work can be performed in this locality by an irresponsible set of white Arabs because the climate is such that they can sleep out doors better than in the house, and they can mess together with a Chinaman for cook, and fare sumptuously with very little house room. The fences that were built before the "no fence bill" became a law, are mostly standing. There are in some localities wheat that would not pay for cutting; this makes excellent pasturage, and the fences are convenient for this purpose. Still, much of the farming is done "out of doors," or without being inclosed. Although the heat of the sun upon this vast level would seem to be almost unbearable, a cool breeze is constantly coming in contact with the breath of this great plain. This breeze is manufactured upon the Buttes, a short spur rising out of the plains upon the other side of the Sacramento river. Wherever these hills lift their towering heads they gather a cooling breath to be sent on the wings of the wind to bless the heated plain lying below. The horizon is very brazen and the few white clouds which have strayed from their normal latitude seem to stand perfectly still, in motionless astonishment at the dried appearance of the thirsty landscape.

July.

STOCKTON.

STOCKTON is situated in San Joaquin County, on San Joaquin River; is a town of about thirteen thousand inhabitants; it now ranks third in the State, and bids fair to give race to Sacramento for the second, both in point of population and commercial interest. Stockton is now one of the largest wheat markets in the world, being surrounded by productive wheat growing valleys; vast quantities of this commodity are stored in the city, waiting for shipment or an advance of prices; it is conveyed to San Francisco, from thence it goes forth to all the civilized nations of the earth, to supply the demand for California's superior bread stuffs. It would seem to be policy for the Californians to take advantage of their remarkably early harvest season, and get their wheat to market before other grain growing countries came in for competition; thus save the trouble and expense of storage, with its multiplicity of risk, besides having the use of the money. In climate Stockton is much like Sacramento, damp and malarious winters, and pretty hot summers; although neither place is considered really unhealthy, this is the tendency if disease lingers in the system at all. Persons troubled with what is know as billiousness will seldom prove better in health from either of these localities. My comparisons between Stockton and Sacramento reminds me of the story of the man with three sons, who had only three pieces of property to divide between them: "The eldest son he gave the mill, the second son an ass, the youngest son, poor little Mat, must be contented with the cat." San Francisco gets the railroad mills and the supreme court mill, while poor Sacramento must with the State house be contented-o. This reminds me of another silly little story of the bees who made a contract with the humming bird to find them with honey. They gave their legs, their wings, and pollen basket, and when they nothing more to give the humming bird flew away and left the bees to starve. This is the way that Sacramento has been treated by the Union Pacific Railroad Company. Stockton has the county seat, it has also the asylum for the insane, being the second son mentioned in the old man's legacy. There are two large foundries, three tanneries and one woolen mill. The blankets manufactured at this mill are not surpassed in the State. A paper mill is also in active operation, where a superior quality of heavy wrapping paper is manufactured from tule hay; and they are now experimenting, with a prospect of making a fine quality of printing paper of the same material. There are three dailies published here, one being edited by a woman, and I will say that the gentlemen show themselves not only gallant in their liberal patronage, but prove by their conversation and deportment to be proud of this living evidence of strongmindedness. Stockton is also a city of magnificent distances, it seems to spread all over San Joaquin county; this may be a slight exaggeration. The difficulty is partially overcome by a one-horse railroad, which appears as endless as an unwound skein of yarn. The steel, as the English say, stretches I cannot imagine how far over the endless plain. In a desperate attempt to see the end of this road, I backed out of the neat little car long before the end was reached or visible, for fear that I should not be able, for some hours, to find my lodgings again.

This city has its share of Christian churchs, nearly all denominations being represented; forming nurseries for the growth of individual opinions, and the development of individual character, thereby preventing any class from tyrany by too great concentration of power. The church buildings are fine gray edifices, and only need a little ivy to cover their dusty walls to give them a cool and really attractive appearance. The church bells are remarkably sweet and musical. For the last five years I have scarcely heard the same church bells for three consecutive Sabbaths, consequently have formed the habit of giving thought to the music of the bells as one forms an opinion upon the tones of the different pianos we hear. Saloons flourish in this city as they do in every town and village of this beautiful State. The handsome proprietor and dashing gambler walk side by side, both excellent specimens of humanity, judging by outward appearances; and, indeed, they seem to possess hearts and brains like other men, but have likely been demoralized by their mothers or some other woman; of course the blame must be placed upon the shoulders of some poor defenseless female, whom it seems as if providence, in its wisdom and mercy, had made as a kind of pack horse for the sins of frail unfortunate man. Then there is the blear-eyed whisky bibber, who, with strong drink, has literally cooked the albumen forming the brain, until he might as well be in possession of a leather brain for all the use it is to him. Wretched human creatures, in many instances as offensive as a mangy dog, and with less capacity for self preservation. No wonder the women of the nation have been led to cry aloud in anguish of spirit to our Father in heaven, that he may care for their sons and keep them from the curse of intemperance. I am sure if men felt as much ashamed of this monstrous curse as women do, that petitions would be placed in all the prayer books, to read as follows: Lead us not into the temptation of strong drink. Deliver us from whisky and it baneful results. Keep us from the temptation of treating and being treated; from the society of the dissolute, and from the evils consequent upon losing ones self respect. Spare us the ill will of those who should bless our memory. Finally, save us from the shame and grave of a drunkard. Amen.

September.

THE STATE INSANE, AND THE ASYLUM.

The asylum for the insane is situated about half a mile from the city of Stockton, and is a very attractive looking retreat, being surrounded by beautifully cultivated grounds. White fences running away through the dense shade give it the appearance of a grand old park. There are two separate buildings upon the grounds, one for the male, the other for the female department; they are located some distance apart; both are built of red brick. The male department has been standing twenty years or more. The walls are covered with green ivy and creeping vines, forming a fine contrast of colors with the red brick. The walks are also of red square brick, the color heightened by frequent washings, for they are kept scrupulously neat. The shade of the front yard is so dense, that, upon entering from the warm, sunny street, one is liable to take a chill, as from the air of a subterraneous cavern. Every thing about the interior of the building appeared cleanly and wholesome. Many of the inmates, in the habit of living at the wretched hotels in this State, have made a change for the better. I learned from the superintending physician that the insane are not so much more numerous in this State than in others as has generally been understood. This institution takes the place of a State almshouse to a certain extent, there being no poor houses except in San Francisco. In this way each county places its poor at the expense of the State unless they are sick; in that case the county hospital is provided for them. There are many at the insane asylum who are only feeble minded, and some idiots who cannot be cared for at home are brought here; many of these in other States would be taken to the county house. Thus, the number *reported* insane in this State greatly exceeds that of others of the same population. The mountaineers or early miners of this country, who have never made homes for themselves, as age creeps on and they get unable to work, must be cared for by the State. This is one particularly sad feature of the settlement of this country. Men who left their homes in the East more than twenty years ago, many middle aged at the time, nearly all with the hope of bettering themselves pecuniarily, and of returning or of sending for their loved ones when able. Some have found the years rolling on and only bringing disappointment, until their children in distant lands have grown to man's and woman's estate, with scarcely an idea of the existence of a father, and with no appreciation of his love or struggles for them. Many have heartlessly deserted their little ones and left them to the fates, or to be brought up by the wretched mother, with all the disadvan tages under which women labor, physically, socially and politically.

There is nothing that will sadden and harden the young heart more than the realization of being deserted, in helpless infancy or inexperienced youth, by those who should have been its protectors. It is bad enough for grown people to live in the world unloved and friendless, but what a sorrow to the heart of the unsophisticated child! Verily, these men have their reward! Being deprived of the society of one's children while they are young is a loss which no human heart can well afford; and the older one gets the more dependent they are upon the young for entertainment and society, aside from the common dependencies of a physical nature. The society of "Old Pioneers" is an association that will benefit some, but many are too far gone to seek protection from organized charity, and must end their days in public institutions. There is something in this apparently indulgent climate that seems to make men reckless. They can live so close to nature without being persecuted by Jack Frost, that if they once get a sniff of mountain air or a taste of wild life, a certain per cent. will turn barbarians in spite of all former ties. I have seen them when they had lost nearly all resemblance to a civilized human being, and appeared more like an old mangy dog than like a man. I am inclined to think man more dependent upon woman for manhood and general usefulness than women upon men, notwithstanding my education to the contrary.

Old women will generally keep themselves tidy and clean, and old maids are proverbial for their neatness. The men about the insane asylum look cleanly and appear contented; all ages are represented. In the male department I saw a toddling infant about a year old; I do not think it was a crazy baby, although it was an inmate of the institution. The female department is a fine large structure, the grounds and improvements comparitively new, but very promising. I approached an elderly gentlemen who was watering the garden, and remarked that "I hoped, in time, to see the grounds about the female department looking as well as they did about the male department. That we women were growing very watchful and fearfully jealous." "Be jabers," said he, "women have no more rights nor men. I likes to see women keep in their proper places; I don't go a cint on these strong minded women; not a cint." Said I to him, "I am a strong minded woman and you have got to stand it; I do not care a cent for weak minded men who presume to venture an opinion upon a subject which they cannot possibly comprehend; and I am going to run for Congress, and you will have to stand that also." At this unexpected disclosure, an indulgent smile of admiration lighted up the countenance of the Hibernian. He had met with such prompt and spirited opposition that it struck him as being very ridiculous that he should be sparring with a lady visitor, and also an aspirant for Congress, and in spite of his severity he wished me success, and hallooed out as I was disappearing, "Good luck to you, miss, be jabers, good luck to you." This was without doubt satire, but what of the braying of a donkey, whether he pays his compliments or calls for his oats, it sounds the same and is void of reason or articulation. There is scarcely a day of my life that I am not reminded of the growth of arrogance, fostered by an atmosphere of political and consequent social injustice. The masculine barbarian is at liberty to fling the unmeaning cant of social prejudice in the face of the most intelligent person in the land, if that person should chance to be a woman. If men could reason with sufficient clearness to understand that these expressions arise from overrating brute force, and underrating other and more important virtues, they would get ashamed to give utterance to such shallow and proverbial canting nonsense. Why should man set himself up as a dictator over his betters when he has nothing more to recommend him than sex, or the fact that he is a male biped? Suppose some illiterate old washerwoman should advise Henry Ward Beecher, or any priest or minister, as to his place in society, and his duties in that particular sphere. How ridiculous it would seem. There is not a demented old scrub of a woman in America but that would exercise better sense.

There is nothing that will make a class of people appear more idiotic than to have more power than they are justly entitled to, and be permitted to manufacture their own reasons without fear of contridiction or criticism. I have learned, by the observation of years, that few men possess the capacity to reason; being controlled almost entirely by their instincts, and many times those sunk lower than the brute by every conceivable selfish abuse. A woman's intuition will tell her the difference between a cultivated man and a boor, while the ignorant man measures all women in one half-bushel, as a donkey would his turnips. A donkey would not have the least idea that turnips could grow for any other purpose than to fill his individual half-bushel, or that of some other donkey's.

As I approached the apartment for women, I could hear a pleasant hum of little noises proceeding from the grated windows, like the sound of numerous birds in a cage. Woman will talk even when sick. This is partly owing to the fact of her having no real business life or business education, as men have. It may be partly constitutional, but I do not believe it. When men go out into the world to do for themselves, they learn silence from many necessities, for fear of giving offense by expressing themselves too freely, and because business cannot be transacted and the mind distracted at the same time with conversation. Where women are educated to business habits or literature, they despise as thoroughly small talk, shallow twaddle, and vulgar inquisitiveness as a corresponding class of men do. The only objectionable feature that I observed about this institution was the cemetery unpleasantly near the female department, in sight of many of its windows. This was located before the female department was planned; has fifteen hundred interred therein, and is too near for such unpleasant associations. I suppose in due course of agitation cremation will become fashionable, and then this place will be summer fallowed and sowed to barley, and the barley sold to the distillers to be used as food for city cows, in order to increase the rates of infant mortality and to propagate insanity. Alas for Dio Lewis and all his plans! This little comparison is much like the way society is tinkered up. All well enough, all well meaning; but while we are watching the enemy upon one side of life's enclosure, he creeps stealthily upon us from some other point. The human family seem like a vast growth of vegetation, so many doomed to die early, some to be blighted but still cling to life, some to be crushed beneath unscrupulous feet never to rise again, and all eventually return to the common mother earth, and there be resolved into the primitive elements. Death must be as much a blessing as any part of the wondrous plan, and the fear or dread of it only a protecting instinct.

As I passed around the institution, an elderly woman called from an upper window: "Good morning, lady." I returned the salutation, and would have been pleased to have held a confab with her, but reflected that this would be violating a rule of the institution, and walked away with a feeling that the unfortunate are fortunate in some respects, by having a place of retirement where they may recover and go out to some usefulness and happiness, or remain and wear out shattered nature until she sinks to eternal rest.

NAPA.

NAPA, the county seat of Napa county, is delightfully situated—far enough from the sea to escape the chilling ocean winds, and of sufficient altitude to have a fine, clear, bracing atmosphere. There are heavy dews at all seasons of the year, and persons seldom take cold in its healthful climate, but going into San Francisco will give almost any outside resident a cold in the head, or upon the lungs. There is something in the humid air of the city that will cause most persons to do some vigorous sneezing before they learn to watch the necessities of the body. Napa has about three thousand inhabitants. Its surroundings are hilly and beautiful as a wall hung with fine paintings of landscape scenery. In a ravine where the public reservoir is located are masses of rock standing like a grand old castle in dignified decay, as if gazing with silent contempt upon the more perishable portions of the mighty structure. A family of Scotch people living near, with their flocks and herds, have christened these towering peaks "Scott's Craig," and say that it resembles Sterling Castle in Scotland. The waters of this ravine are imprisoned in a reservoir and watched by these hardened old sentinels, which stand guard in such an attitude that it would not be surprising if one craig should lose its balance and tumble over to the entire destruction of every perishable thing upon its downward course. There is much grape-growing and wine-making in this valley, as well as other industrial enterprises. I visited Wordard's wine-making establishment, and found at work about fifteen foreigners of various nationalities engaged in making wine. I interrogated one of them as to the probability of his tiring of the sameness of his occupation. He answered in broken English that he was "born in wine," and knew nothing else. A portion of this statement I had no reason to doubt. In this cellar there is about fifty thousand gallons of wine, the most aged being five years old. Napa has two tanneries in working order. B. F. Sawyer & Co. work in about three hundred sheepskins in a day and one hundred deerskins. This is made into glove leather, leather for linings, etc. The wool from this tannery forms quite a feature in the business; it is pulled, washed, dried and sold in the Boston market for forty cents per pound. Wheat is extensively raised in this county, as well as everything else needed for the comfort and sustenance of man and beast in a semi-tropical climate. I was much interested in seeing a boat loaded with this commodity from a warehouse. These boats run up a river known as Napa creek, which empties into San Pueblo Bay. All these rivers and streams in the vicinity of the ocean are affected by the ocean tides, the waters usually being very brakish from the close proximity to the sea, and shallow when tide is low or out, and high enough for simple navigation when tide is in. While one of these little crafts was being loaded, a dear old mother cat and two half-grown kittens were lending their assistance. The removal of a bag was watched with the greatest possible interest, and woe to the mouse or rat that was unhoused in the presence of these faithful servants. I was told that they work all day with the men as diligently as any hand in the building.

A branch of the insane asylum is located at Napa. Two hundred and fifty thousand dollars were appropriated by the State Legislature in 1871. The last session there was another appropriation of six hundred and thirty thousand dollars. The building is not yet finished and more money must be voted before it can be. It would seem for so young a State as California that she is going to a vast amount of expense to build public institutions for future generations. Considering that there is a mighty national debt caused by the calamities incident upon war, one would think that in all wisdom this State would forego for the present the building of expensive structures until the wealth of the country was more fully developed and there was a larger population to stand the tax and to share the expenditure. An unhealthy love of display has taken such a hold upon the people of this county that it is as apparent in their public as private lives. There are many worthy institutions in San Francisco which are suffering for want of means while we have a State house, an insane asylum, and a city hall that would do credit to the oldest and most densely populated State in the Union. Iowa legislated for her industrious population in a very plain brick building, which cost less than many a private residence; and not until they were clear of debt, and had a surplus fund in the treasury, did they talk of a new State house. Property in California is taxed at its real value, while in the Northwestern States it is taxed at but one-third its value. These large tracts of land held by speculators, by some political chicanery escape taxaation almost entirely. It is an indisputable fact that the mass of people in this State are much poorer than in the older or Western States. There is not the thrift among them, they are too heavily taxed for the amount of wealth developed, and these expensive institutions sap the life from the living industries of the country. The branch insane asylum at Napa has an appropriation of two hundred and eight acres of land. The building is much larger than either of the departments at Stockton. The brick used in this structure is made upon the ground. There is a patch of clay upon a neighboring place of which the brick is made; and, strange to say, this purpose will exhaust the material, and there is no more to be found for miles around. The brick cost nine dollars and seven and a half cents per thousand. The basement is made of stone, a material to be found in abundance in the foot-hills. A fine stone for ornamental purposes is manufactured upon the ground; Freer's patent is used. The sand of which this stone is composed is brought from England, being used by wheat vessels as ballast, as they go hence heavily laden and return comparatively empty; and as there is no further need of this ballast when the vessels come into port, they dispose of it at a very low figure, and it is mixed with Portland cement, placed in wooden forms, and made any desired shape or size, as we would mould butter. Those beautiful caps for doors, windows, and cornices, are made in this way, and when dry are solid, to all appearance, as the natural granite from the hills. The asylum is built in sections or wings, and will have seven round towers made fire-proof, and placed in certain angles, so that in case of conflagration the destroying element could not spread to the adjacent parts of the structure. These towers, besides giving an air of magnificence to the entire edifice, will be used for elevators. There is a chapel for religious worship, and an elegant billiard room adjoining. This structure is four stories in height, is heated with hot air, and the water coming from the mountain reservoir has sufficient head to reach the upper stories with surplus force. It is well ventilated, and provided with screens for the doors and windows, so that insinuating insects cannot enter. The culinary and laundry departments are separate from the building, connecting with the main part by an underground railroad or tunnel. The only thing about the plan of this institution that I did not indorse was the fact that the cemetery is located upon the same ground and inconveniently near. This is a fearful oversight which the committee should rectify before too late, unless they anticipate the age of cremation. The white stones of a cemetery point downwards as well as upwards, and persons suffering physical and mental infirmities can scarce afford to have these ghostly reminders constantly in sight.

Notwithstanding that Napa is a beautiful place and has so many natural advantages, the people seem lacking in gentlemen to serve the county as officials. The district attorney is a most pitiable creature, who expressed himself as fearfully jealous of the subject of woman's anticipated citizenship, and mentioned Susan B. Anthony as "a superannuated old hag." It is evident by those who comprehend the subject, that nothing but power will command respect. I am daily assured by the language of the usurper that if women remain quietly submitting in all things to the will of the master that she shall be respected. No woman with any sense worth mentioning, desires to be respected upon such conditions; we intend to chose our own modes of commanding respect; power will always bring this; and while man may be venerated for being the larger animal, woman should be respected for the balance of political power.

NOVEMBER.

LAKE TAHOE.

LEAVING Colfax by the freight train, I find myself once more passing through the Central Pacific's lengthy snow sheds. With the return of spring portions of these structures are removed in order to prevent the spread of fire, and the builders seem to have made use of a variety of plans, as no two tiers of shedding appear to be constructed after the same. In passing one plan of construction, the sun comes pouring through a thousand apertures, striking the train while in motion, giving it the appearance of being showered with golden sun balls, sparkling like falling rockets. In another plan the sun strikes the train in a rapidly moving checkerboard, and the effect is really quite wonderful and very pleasing. One must ride in the elevated seat of the caboose of the freight train in order to view this novel feature of the snow sheds. While the train stopped to water, I alighted to see a cinnamon bear, tied in an enclosure at the station. Upon the wall near by there hung a huge parrot cage covered by a gunny sack, and upon the sack was written in large letters, "This cage contains a monstrous Red Bat, of an hitherto unknown species, discovered and captured upon a lofty peak of the Sierra Nevada mountains." As a matter of course I wanted to see the great Red Bat, but did not dare lift the gunny sack for fear the creature might be vicious, so I walked into the office of the hotel and requested the polite, handsome clerk to show me the Bat. He seemed delighted to be of the least service in a matter of scientific interest; his countenance fairly glowed with the pleasure of serving, as he thrust his pen over his ear and strutted out. I had never seen a hotel clerk more radient, and thought to myself if these fellows only knew what an adornment politeness is to hotel clerks, they would wear more of it and less jewelry. I was so overcome by this unusual display of suavity, that I had a great mind to order my baggage off the train and stay long enough to study the singular phenomenon in the person of the clerk. By this time we had reached the cage. The gunny sack was carefully raised that I might not suffer a nervous shock at the first sight of the monster. I placed my hands securely under my bustle and peeped cautiously in, when to my horror and surprise there was nothing to be seen but a piece of red brick with a string tied around the center, and it suspended in the middle of the cage. The whistle blew and I hurried aboard the train without even stopping to thank the handsome clerk, although I managed to wave my hand at him through the window, and to receive in return the smiling adieus of quite an audience of spectators, and without doubt sympathizers, for they had all peeped under the gunny sack. But upon mature reflection, I rather enjoyed the joke, although it was a little wicked.

Tourists stop over night at the Truckee Hotel, and the next morning take the stage for a ride of fourteen miles to Lake Tahoe. This route like those at the Yosemite, is so finely shaded that the drive is like passing through an elegant park. The sugar pine is missing here, it does not condescend to live only in certain localities. The foliage of these evergreens stand so luxuriently against the clear blue sky, that they appear more like carved work, heavy mosses, or trimming loaded with heavy green beads, than simple foliage. In this altitude, the weight of the winter snows bend the young limbs, giving them the appearance of having just divested themselves of this extra weight, leaving them with a peculiar Lapland grace. The edges of the boughs are pushing out fresh leaves, consequently the limbs are fringed upon the extremities with a light shade of the most delicate green. The atmosphere is perfumed with the medicinal fragrance of the elecampane and mountain sage. Occasionally there may be seen a yellow butter cup, bending low to touch the limpid waters of the running rivulet.

The stage driver upon this route is an intelligent specimen of the Jehu fraternity as one often meets; his name is Adams, a decendant, without doubt, of old father Adam. Many were the places of interest he pointed out, and his anecdotes were related with a tenderness of sentiment that caused my eyes to water occasionally, notwithstanding I had my sun glasses along with me. A dark, lonely ravine, overshadowed with pines, was pointed out as having a sad history associated with it. A man came here and located a piece of land, built him a hut and lived in hermit like isolation. At last his means were exhausted, discouragements came, and in a fit of insanity he committed suicide. An acquaintance walked two or three miles to see him, owing to his frame of mind when last out, and found him lying upon the floor, with a ball through his head, and a pistol at his side. The poor fellow was not yet dead, and when questioned as to who did it, answered that he did not know who did. His condition was such that nothing more intelligible could be elicited, and as he died shortly after, it is supposed that he did not know what he was saying. His answer caused some uneasiness as to whether he had not been murdered by some other hand than his own. A coroner's inquest was held and the jury decided that it was a case of suicide, and the body was taken to the Hot Spring Hotel, and from there buried upon the banks of the beautiful Tahoe. Pitying hands have placed a rude paling about the little mound, and the lofty pines lower their heads and sigh mournfully above it. The grave of this poor suicide occupies a more conspicuous place than did the living man, and will probably be the subject of more heartfelt sympathy and interest, even from the pleasure seeking tourist, than the last resting place of many a celebrated hero.

A few rods futher on is another mound enclosed with a painted paling. This is the grave of a consumptive who came from his home in the East, hoping to be benefitted by the climate; but in his case nature had given up trying, and he requested to be laid upon the banks of Tahoe, preferring the sunny hill side of the Golden State for his last sleep, to the frost bound home of his childhood. Adams gave me the benefit of several anecdotes, two of which I will relate, as the disposition of the narrator is so very apparent in both.

There was an old man camping in these woods

and he owned a donkey, which appeared to be a veteran also. The two had just returned from an expedition in quest of supplies. The donkey was tied to a tree while the owner busied himself gathering faggots for the camp fire. A hunter came stealing softly down the hill and caught sight of the donkey's back, and thinking it was a grizzly bear, drew his rifle and shot the poor creature through. The donkey was not killed dead, and it is said that it could be heard to roar at an almost incredible distance. The old man was nearly frantic, not only at the pecuniary loss which he was poorly able to bear, but from the death of a creature that had been his faithful servant and only companion for years. When the hunter came to learn his mistake, his feelings can better be imagined than described. He paid the old man for his donkey, and earnestly requested that nothing be said about the matter, as he was a candidate for some political office.

As to the other story, Adams was himself one of the express company. Several men had set out upon an expedition over the mountains, taking pack animals, intending to spend a few days in the open air. There came a heavy fall of snow, and the campers were detained until they run short of provisions, and there was some danger of their perishing before they could reach a settlement. They had among the pack animals a young gelding donkey. The creature was a short-legged little dump, very fat, with a remarkable amiable disposition, and a great pet by all who knew him. He was called Little Jim, and it was found quite impossible for the short-legged little creature to keep pace with the other animals in the deep snow, although he would hold his own wonderfully with an ordinary chance. His pack was removed to the back of another animal, and he was led in the trail made by the rest, and everything done to equalize things; but there was no use, the train were obliged to stop often for Little Jim to come up, or he would have been left hopelessly behind to perish in the snow. When the men had been without food for two days, and the prospects were that two more might elapse before a settlement could be reached, one of the company, more desperate than the rest, proposed that they kill Little Jim and make steak of him. At first the men cast sidelong glances at one another, as if ashamed of the thought, and at last commenced to discuss the matter. After listening to an argument in which Jim's disabilities were ably set forth, the owner gave a sorrowful consent that the creature should be slain to save the lives of himself and companions. They cast lots as to who should fire the shot that was to bring Jim to his death, mercifully excluding the name of the owner, as he said that he would never raise his hand to take the life of a creature that he had fed and reared, and that placed unlimited confidence in him. This excuse was accepted, and poor Little Jim fell by the hand of another. Said the narrator, I could see a change come over the countenances of the men the moment they heard the crack of the rifle, as if this was indeed a desperate measure. They skinned the hind quarters of the donkey and cooked it like steak, declaring it to be the sweetest, tenderest, juciest meat that they had ever eaten, far surpassing the steak of beef; and to this day they still assert that their prejudice in favor of donkey beef was certainly not entirely the results of ravenous hunger. My narrator here added that they all felt like murderous cowards for killing Little Jim, and that the comforts of justification only came to their relief by a consciousness of this measure having saved their lives, for it was two days more before they reached the settlement. Alas, poor Jim! and I brushed a tear from my glasses as we drove up to the Hot Spring Hotel.

The people came out of the house *en masse* to greet the new comers. Among the members of the household was a dear little fawn, about two months and a half old. It seemed to realize the fact that it had some new acquaintances to make or that it had discovered an old one in my buckskin gloves, for I was not long in finding out that the creature had not been weaned. A tourist stopping at the hotel had a couple of very fine dogs, one an Italian greyhound, the other a black and tan. These dogs would weigh about five pounds apiece, and were understood to be "heavy dogs." Tan was very fond of chasing the fawn, always taking the lead in every enterprise, while the hound would follow any example. For a while the chase was nice sport, and the fawn seemed to enjoy it as well as the dogs. At last it became annoying, and the little deer would seek refuge beside some one, as if soliciting protection. She was standing by my side, watching the movements of the dogs with much apparent anxiety, and I said, "Fawny, why don't you strike the dogs with your feet," (at the same time making a gesture,) "that would make them keep quiet." I had hardly finished speaking when Tan came up, barking furiously, expecting the deer to run, when to my astonishment the fawn leaped forward, striking the dog a hard blow with her little sharp hoof. Those who saw it were both amused and surprised, for the hotel proprietor said it was her first attempt at self-defense, and it appeared as if she had taken my advice instantly. The fawn looked about as if she thought that was just the right thing, while the poor sensitive little dog was evidently the most astonished and humiliated creature living. As everybody laughed, he did not seem to expect any sympathy, and lay down where he could keep an eye upon the creature whose graceful movements had so delighted his little dog's heart; and the glances which he cast about plainly showed what he was thinking of, and when any person spoke to him he licked his little foot in silence, still looking at the fawn as if he could not believe his senses. The two dogs never after offered to give chase to the fawn.

Now for the first time I walk out upon the wharf to take a look at the matchless waters of Lake Tahoe. I can only express myself in exclamations. The water is so clear that one can see to the depth of fifty feet any object that is visible at that distance in the open air. When at a distance from the lake I had not been much impressed with its superiority over other bodies of water. To be sure the green, purple, blue and white lines were rather wonderful; but one must get acquainted with this delightful sheet of water to appreciate it. The lake is thirty-six miles in length and fifteen in width; lies partly in the Golden and partly in the Silver State; is literally cradled in the Sierra Nevada mountains, six thousand four hundred feet above the level of the sea. All along the northern shore there are springs of boiling hot water coming to the surface, containing lime, magnesia, sulphur. The hot baths are delightful, the water possessing just the requisite properties for cleansing both the cuticle and all kinds of clothing. One comes from the bath as white and pure as a new kid glove. Notwithstanding these hot springs, which can be seen boiling up between sheets of melted lava, the body of the lake water is extremely cold. No animal life exists except that which is indigent to northern latitudes. There are plenty of trout, whitefish and salmon trout, I am told. The trout do not stroll about alone, but are always seen in shoals. A finny community of these graceful fishes is one of the most beautiful sights associated with these transparent waters. The water is so clear from foreign substance, so cold and void of insect life, that it is a wonder how the fishes manage to subsist. No vegetation is seen growing in any part of this lake, the bottom being melted lava or rocks. Dead fishes are occasionally seen lying upon their backs, showing no signs of decay. Nearly all the fish seen dead are about the same age --- two years old. Since trout farming has become a business it is an easy matter to understand the age of a trout by its size. I am wondering if the trout cut a new set of teeth, or develop fresh fins or gills, that tax their vitality at a certain age, causing unusual mortality among them. The fish farmers ought to know.

There have been thirteen human lives lost upon this water within a few years; not a body has ever been recovered. It is supposed that, the water being so cold, no gasses form, and the bodies are preserved, never rising to the surface. Upon this lake there is a beautiful little steamer, of sixty-four tons burden, drawing about three feet of water. This boat wears the brand of the Central Pacific Railroad, as nearly everything does upon the Pacific coast, being called the Governor Stanford. At eight o'clock every morning this steamer leaves Hot Spring wharf for Tahoe City and all the points of interest upon the lake. The day I took passage quite an event occurred, and as said event was productive of no immediate serious results, of course it caused much amusement to the spectators. A tourist from San Francisco, entirely unaccustomed to the water, and ignorant of the philosophy of navigation, jumped from the wharf into the stern of a small row boat; of course the boat shot from under the astonished landsman, and left him splashing in twenty feet of transparent water. The man could not swim, and was rescued by the bar-keeper of the place, who it seems has another mission besides that of mixing mint juleps and cocktails. The ambitious tourist retired from sight amid the plaudits of the spectators, who of course were congratulating him upon his timely rescue, not making sport of his foolhardy enterprise. In a reasonable length of time a gentleman's outfit could be seen dangling in a limp manner from one of the dormer windows in the hotel.

From Hot Springs to Tahoe City the distance is nearly ten miles, and is a most enchanting voyage. The water is so clear that it is impossible to detect the surface except by the ripples made by the steamer, or in case some foreign substance should chance to be borne along on the surface; and leaning over the side of the steamer gave one the impression of being propelled through the air. The boat was not heavily loaded, and seemed to glide upon the surface like a bird. The agitation caused by the movement of the boat made a most charming picture, giving the steamer the appearance of being trimmed with white and pearl-gray lace upon a deep blue satin background, thickly spangled with silver buttons. The water is blue as indigo where it is over a hundred feet deep, and green as a piece of beautiful green silk where it is only fifty and seventy-five feet. Where the green and blue waters join a line of the most delicate purple is the result; and the reason the beautiful tints are so fine and distinct is because of the water being so perfectly pure. No person can conceive or imagine the perfection of color and its wonderful beauty without first beholding it. There are places which are known as beyond the soundings, where the water is so deep that exquisite blue and violet is turned to a blue-black, and is called the black waters. Where the water is fifty feet deep we are shown the coral beds, so called from their resemblance to coral, but really beds of pumice stone, which have been for ages subject to the action of volcanic fires, and at last settled down, been overcome by another element, become the bed of a lake which is decidedly cool; and when earth's changes shall drain Tahoe of its crystal waters, it will leave something such a valley as Yosemite, minus, however, the grand rocky formation of that valley. The shadow of the smoke coming from the steamer could be seen at the depth of fifty feet as plainly as if it had fallen upon a board walk.

Thus far I have been so enchanted with the waters of this lake that I have entirely overlooked the surroundings, almost forgotten that it had any; but it lies in a fairy land, being enclosed in an unbroken chain of hills covered with brown and fringed with mountain pines. The distance around the lake is about one hundred miles; but at intervals all along the shores are public houses, giving accommodations to the tourist in a variety of locations. There are stage lines, post-offices and telegraph lines in all directions. Beautiful women and children, in gay dresses, are seen playing croquet, swinging, and participating in all manner of outdoor games, fishing and hunting pebbles, for there are no little shells to be gathered on these shores. The angle worms used for bait are brought from Chicago, and sold to the sporting tourist.

In this faultless climate there are no storms of wind or rain, nor intense heat to prostrate or interfere with one's plans by the day, week, or for the summer campaign. The woods are alive with people camping out for the benefit of the mountain atmosphere; and many avail themselves of this sight-seeing who could hardly stand the trip as taken by the tourist, with the expense of public locomotion and that of living at hotels. It certainly takes cares outside of climatic influence in California to create in man a compensating wretchedness.

In our steamboat route we pass a place known as Emerald Bay. Here, in one view, the blue water, the violet and the most exquisite green, all come before the sight in rotation. It seemed to me that the waters of this bay, and the hills around must be peopled with spirits, faries, or some unearthly beings. One realizes that this lake lies near heaven; it is the only way to satisfy the imagination in regard to its unearthly colors and indescribable beauty. Ben Halliday has a summer residence upon the banks of these fairy waters, and here an old sailor made a grave and built a tomb for himself, and to show the uncertainty of things in this life, even in death, he was never buried at all, but lost at sea. Beyond this point of interest there is a bluff rising perpendicular from the water's edge three or four hundred feet, and the water is said to be a hundred feet deep at its base. Crossing over from Emerald Bay to this bluff is termed spanning the Rubicon. Just around one point there is standing a rough stone image, which a little stretch of the imagination will convert into a grizzly, sitting on his haunches, with paws drooping. This image certainly bears more resemblance to a grizzly than it does to a donkey, and in return for politeness rendered me once upon a time, I propose to call it Governor Stanford, after the little steamboat of that name. Here the whistle of the steamer was sounded that the passengers might listen to the echo.

Further on we were shown a cave, a singularly conspicuous formation, standing with its entrance very properly toward the lake. It stands alone at the foot of the hills, upon the bank, as if for the convenience of water; is a mass, I should think, seventy-five or a hundred feet in height, having the general outline of an old-fashioned mud oven; the entrance is shaped like the mouth of an oven and is said to lead to a room thirty feet deep. Some of the gods may have done their baking in this locality while planning the design for Tahoe and experimenting upon its exquisite colors. At Glenbrook, a lumbering point, the steamer ties up for the night. Here we fully realize that this beautiful lake can be desecrated by practical uses. Logs are made into rafts and floated upon its limped waters; mills are built upon its banks; hard-handed laborers work about its fairy precincts, looking like any thing but angels, although they may become such when they lay off their buff-colored overalls and being baptized in the purifying waters of Tahoe; it may be so, I decline to be their judge. In this altitude there is frost every month in the year; the consequence is that few persons will make permanent residence, as nothing but cabbages, potatoes, and such vegetation as frost does not injure, can be raised with any degree of certainty. The snow falls very deep in winter, although it is not cold, but the time is coming when many of the hotels will be kept open all winter as the population increases and there is a demand for winter resorts for invalids, for the air of this region is as pure as its waters. I tarried for the night in a comfortable country hotel, situated in the edge of a delightful forest of pines, and took the little steamer at seven in the morning, and at eight had made the round of the lake and returned to Hot Spring Hotel. Here I learned that another tourist had fallen off the wharf while experimenting with a boat and was rescued by the same man. This made three persons — one boy of nine years, and two men who had taken a plunge-bath in one week from the same point, and all rescued by the little bar tender, who is known as "Shorty." If this man keeps on in this way he certainly should receive a medal from some organization of a humanitarian nature. The society formed for preventing cruelty to animals should recognize him in absence of any other; for man is certainly an animal, and at times manifesting sufficient greenness to almost be claimed as a vegetable. This water is so distilled from all foreign particles that it is extremely light, making it difficult for swimmers to keep up, and the lightness of the air in this altitude may have something to do with the difficulty of swimming. Logs, timber, boards, and corked bottles go to the bottom. There is a rumor to the effect that the railroad company intend some day to tunnel the mountain at this point to save the vast yearly expenditure for snow sheds. If this tunneling is ever accomplished, it will be an easy matter to conduct the waters of Lake Tahoe to the cities of Sacramento, San Jose, and San Francisco, furnishing them with the best water in the world. Then an extra pipe could be laid from the Hot Springs, thus giving them water for cleansing purposes that if properly used would cleanse the dirty pool of politics. Sacramento would have occasion to rejoice, San Jose to be more exquisite, and San Francisco to be glad, as this prepared water would make a wonderful saving in soap, besides giving unlimited means of purification. These cities could then have public baths, so that the poorest paid laborer would have an opportunity to cleanse his cuticle, and grow in purity of character in proportion to personal cleanliness. The "Muldoons" and "Hoodlums" would then come into the presence of his honor, the police judge, with clean faces, and society would be revolutionized for the better. When all this is brought about by the money and enterprise of the Central Pacific Railroad Co., I am ready to forgive them for being a powerful grasping monopoly.

FISH FARMING AT LAKE TAHOE.

Pingel, Morgan & Hurly are the names of the men composing the firm engaged in the business of pisciculture at Tahoe City. This is comparatively a new business, and the public must be interested in anything written upon this subject, at least until it is better understood. As this lake lies partly in the State of California and partly in Nevada, those States have passed acts protecting the fish, making it an offense to catch them with seins at any season of the year. Farming companies are however permitted to draw them with the sein for their spawn, returning the fish uninjured to the water again, as will presently be understood. The first of April the male fish starts up the tributaries, it is supposed to find a suitable place for the female to spawn. The fact that the male goes first to prepare the way was ascertained by the first hauls that were made proving mostly male fish; of course they produced no spawn and it was found upon experimenting that the fish must be caught later in the season in order to obtain equal numbers of both sexes. A little later the male returns to the lake, takes his mate, and the two start off together, continuing their course up the stream until the water is so shallow that they can barely live. Here the female deposits the spawn and the male passes over it, leaving the semen. It is said that the male defends the eggs, gallantly fighting, and doing his best to keep away the villainous fishes which always follow these pilgrims on purpose to eat the spawn.

> Who taught the little fish the way
>   Her finny course to steer,
> To search out inland cove and bay,
>   And guard her young with fear?

The sein is spread at the mouth of the stream to catch them as they are going up, and they are captured by thousands. They are then placed in a creel, made of slats an inch in width and half an inch apart. This creel is shaped much like a large coffin, having a little trap door at the top. The fish are taken from the net and put into the creel, which lies partly under water. This is then brought alongside a small pier and the fishes taken up by a scoop-net and put into a pail. Here the females are squeezed until they emit about a hundred of their eggs, and the males are served the same, emitting a small quantity of semen. The fishes are then returned to the lake to resume their propagating pilgrimage without injury or further interruption. The vessel containing the spawn is permitted to stand a few minutes, being once stirred about; the impregnation is then complete, and the eggs are placed in shallow troughs six inches or a foot in width and ten feet long. These boxes are placed upon an inclined plane and covered by shedding, thus shading them from the sun. The coldest water to be obtained, even ice water, is permitted to trickle over the spawn until they are hatched. The exact time which it takes the eggs to hatch I did not ascertain. The age of fishes can now be obtained as accurately as any other creature. Seventy-five per cent. of the eggs are hatched by this process. The colder the water the longer they will be in coming forth, but the hardier. Fishes hatched in warmer water are not as liable to live. When first hatched the minnows are about half an inch in length, as lively as crickets, and for several days they carry upon their backs the belicose sack, which looks like a beech tree bud when it first begins to swell in the spring of the year. The creatures appear wonderfully funny, moving rapidly about with a little pink sack upon their backs. When leaving the spawning boxes they are put into another small trough of running water, and kept for a few weeks; then placed into deep ponds ten or twelve feet across, where they are able to hide from the sun. The trout is eminently a cold-water fish, seeking the deep shady nooks and quiet pools of the coldest mountain streams. The fishes of one pond are all of one age; this precaution is necessary to keep them from eating one another. The trout is a rascally cannibal; having a great mouth he can swallow a fish nearly as large as himself. They are fed with finely minced meat, and it is a very nice sight to see them jump and scramble over one another like chickens, when coming for food. They manifest as much intelligence as birds do, and the keeper said he became very much attached to them. The keeper had a little scoop-net with which he touched the water; they thinking there was food came once, but could not be deceived again, for they did not come out until there were pieces of meat visible. At seven weeks old they are little over an inch in length; at one year old they are about six inches; at two, eight; at five years old, fifteen inches in length, and quite a fish, weighing two and a half or three pounds. Judging from the size, many of these fishes live to be ten, fifteen and twenty years of age. This fish farm is about five years old, is a success financially. The fishes are sold for supplying aquariums; also for food. Many tourists, ladies and children, think it a very nice thing to go a trouting, and for a consideration they are permitted to try their skill at angling in these ponds. The fishes are so tame that they can be scooped up in numbers with the hand net. The white fish is a pleasant feature of these ponds. Those that I saw were about a foot in length, of a light transparent gray color, with beautiful bright silver dots upon their sides. The white fish has no cannibalistic tendencies; he is a scavenger, grubbing at the bottom of the pond for his living. He has a small round mouth, projecting like the snout of a pig, and surrounded with a cartilageous ring something like the rooter of the swine, and two little fins appear about where the ears should be, making him look still more piggy, and to complete the resemblance, he actually roots the dirt upon the bottom as he passes along, champing swineishly. The waters of Tahoe are so transparent that its inhabitants, the fishes, might as well live in glass houses.

CORAL OR ALABASTER CAVE.

THIS natural curiosity is situated in Eldroado county, nine miles north of Auburn, the county seat of Placer county. This cave was discovered the 18th of April, 1860, by some workmen who were excavating in the side of the mountain for a lime kiln. Soon after its discovery it was visited by Starr King, and a party of several persons from San Francisco. Starr King offered up a prayer from the natural pulpit thus dedicating it in a Christian like manner to the general public. At first it was called Coral cave and the register appeared with this heading, but it seems that Alabaster is preferred by the natives, for the latter has succeeded the former, so that it is generally known as Alabaster cave. The floor of the cavern is very irregular and muddy, making it necessary to wear rubber over shoes while exploring. About fifty candles are cut in two, lighted, and placed upon niches and boards upon the floor in order to give the necessary illumination. A large looking glass was also placed at the entrance where the sun could strike it and the reflected light was thrown upon some of the most prominent objects. The whole cavern is about three hundred feet long and a hundred in width in many places, still the different compartments are as haphazard as one would expect in a natural excavation. In some parts it is so low that one is obliged to stoop very much in order to pass, in other places it is ten or twelve feet to the roof, and in two or three instances the roof terminates in a tunnel or funnel, resembling a chimney, but not running up a sufficient distance to open the ground at the top. There are places where the roof seems to be ceiled or inlaid with marble, striped all one way, and with a wonderful variety of colors, and as if the cracks or joints appeared about two feet apart. There are rows of fine stalactites forming a fringe, partaking of the same variety of colors as the marble ceiling. In a dim light one can fancy that it is ornamental papers cut and placed in rows as they are seen in restaurants for fly screens. In some places beautiful stalactites, shaped and colored like tallow candles, hang from the roof and remind me forcibly of the days when our grandmothers dipped candles and hung them in some out of the way room to dry and harden fit for use. Some of these, judging by the tint, seem to have more beeswax in them than others. Many of them were shaped like a carrot, and some exactly the same pale yellow color; an exquisite shade of buff when examined by sun light. Some, from a composition of iron, are tinted with pink. All are dropping tears of a chemical preparation, though not profusely.

There is one beautiful object known as Mrs. Lincoln's pocket handkerchief. It is suspended from the roof like a napkin held in the center, showing two of the corners. There is a line looking like a wide hem, and the whole is as white as a wax lily, and the angles are so perfect that it has the exact appearance of a very elegant handkerchief. There are not many stalagmites in this cavern. Those that are to be seen are formed in lumps looking like sheep, lambs, or animals in repose.

The celebrated pulpit is a huge lump of the dripping chemicals, stalagmitic in formation, situated upon a side elevation, and a dark buff color. The corrugations occurring in most of these objects, gives them the appearance of having been carved or turned in a lathe. There is a singular formation which appears like a beef heart hanging upon a wall. The yellow flakes of tallow usually accompanying the fresh heart of a beef, are upon this object as if it were a work of imitation in art. It is to be regretted that this beautiful curiosity in nature cannot be protected from vandalism. Its stalactites are broken off and carried away; nearly every cabinet on the Pacific coast has a specimen, thus robbing the public of a rare and wonderful treat in the line of natural curiosity.

"SWEET AUBURN."

Auburn, the county seat of Placer county, is a lovely little place of about fifteen hundred

hundred inhabitants. Is located half a mile from the Central Pacific Railroad. It is more enchanting because of its hilly site, its wonderfully healthy climate and dense shade, than from its architectural beauty. The streets are as uncertain in their angles as those of the town of Monterey. The thoroughfares were never laid out in either of these places, but just grew from circumstances. I have a wonderful liking for these mountain towns — they may not be as well for money making operations, but they are more peaceful and quiet than the valley towns. The inhabitants are fairer in complexion, the fruits are finer in flavor, the flowers are more fragrant, in fact they are nearer heaven than the valleys, and while we tarry out of paradise, there is no better place to live and breathe than in these mountain towns of the Golden State.

GOING TO INTO THE YOSEMITE VALLEY.

HOW TO VISIT THE VALLEY TO ADVANTAGE.

FIRST, purchase your tickets of parties most popular in business. The railroad company are reliable and responsible, and as they run nearly everything in this State, must have a share in the pecuniary interests of the Yosemite. In getting your ticket have a fair understanding placed in writing; for if one fails to mention the fact that guides are to be furnished, extra charges will be made in the valley. This little matter has caused much annoyance among tourists; finding that they had paid the price, including guides, but not having the fact stated upon the ticket or in writing, were obliged to pay extra. There is nothing right or just about this mode of transacting business, but it is what some business men term "smart." It is hardly possible for all men to respect themselves too much for such contemptible trickery in business. The route and time for reaching the Yosemite Valley are as follows: The Oakland boat leaves Broadway wharf at four o'clock P. M.; after a trip across the bay you take the train and reach Lathrop's at eight o'clock, here fifteen minutes are allowed for supper; distance from San Francisco eighty-two miles. The hotel at this place is owned by the railroad company. The Thompson brothers, having full control, do everything to please during the limited time one remains; then change cars for Merced; this is the Visalia division of the Central Pacific Railroad. This branch is completed to Calienta, a distance of two hundred and forty-one miles from Lathrop. At Merced remain over night. The hotel here is owned by the railroad company also; is a large commodious wooden building, at present kept by a pig-headed proprietor hardly capable of taking charge of a canal boat, who is so afraid of offending people and losing custom that a set of riotous tourists are permitted to come in and take possession of the house, to sing and tear around all night, while their hunting dogs are kept in the bed-rooms howling a mournful vesper for the benefit of persons who are to ride by stage sixty-eight miles next day. If a traveler has a mind to take the responsibility of saying to them that they shall be arrested for disturbing the peace, he may possibly get an hour's sleep to prepare him for his journey the day following. Many have owed to the incapacity of this hotel proprietor the fact that they were not able to "do" the valley after reaching it.

Stages leave the town of Merced for both the Mariposa and the Coulterville route; the Mariposa daily and the Coulterville tri-weekly. Six o'clock in the morning is the time for starting. It is best to go by the Mariposa route and return by Coulterville, as it gives one just so much more variety. May or June are the best months for visiting this wonder in nature, because of the falls which are made and sustained by the melting snows upon loftier peaks. The valley may be seen with pleasure and advantage at almost any season of the year, but many of those beautiful falls fail during latter part of summer. At present the people can only complain of the little clap-traps organized to get money out of the traveling public. I, for my part, see nothing wrong in the private enterprise of building roads and making trails about the valley, where a small toll is charged. It is certain that this thing would not have been accessible to the public for some time yet, but for the individual's hope of making something. It will be some time now before the State really wakes up to the fact of having this valley to take care of; and still some time before it will work intelligently as to the needs of the public. The lands are leased for the purpose of raising a fund, and it is to be hoped that some firm, strong, rustic bridges will be constructed across its numerous streams; that the roads may be bought of individuals and made free that guides may be paid a salary, the same as the guardian of the valley; that the hotel accommodation shall be such that tourists or invalids may remain any length of time they may choose, instead of being rushed in and out of the valley as if the object was to pick their pockets and let them go. A person going from San Francisco into the valley needs about a hundred and fifty dollars; it may not take more than one hundred and twenty-five, but the first mentioned is the least one should think of doing the valley with and stay a week or ten days. It consumes a whole day to visit any one point of interest in this valley of tears and trickling water-falls. This chapter is written upon going in by the Coulterville route. We pass through several miles of wheat fields and much fine country under cultivation, and cross the swollen river Merced by a ferry. The first place for dinner after leaving the town of Merced, is Lebryghts, a pleasant home where the climbing roses blossom by the door, and we are treated to a bountiful dinner at the price of fifty cents. Most persons can digest but indifferently when traveling rapidly over these roads in a public conveyance. The exercise is too violent for successful assimulation, and a system of fasting is at once imposed upon one. Some invalid food can be used to advantage, such as Imperial granuum, rice, or corn starch, something easily digested; for with many a regular sea-sickness prevails, and still it is wonderful what delicate persons can endure in this mountain air. If one is out of doors much it is almost impossible to be troubled with illness. Many persons visit this valley with their own conveyances and camp out for weeks. It is a nice way to do providing one gets help to perform the physical drudgery of camp life, for there is business enough to give a tourist all the exercise he will desire to take in "doing" the valley. In the afternoon we reach Coulterville, an interesting mountain town of about fifteen hundred inhabitants. The style of architecture attracted much attention in this place, the buildings being nearly all constructed with the low broad gable roof. The material varying from stone, brick, wood, and adobe. The hotel, set in a side hill and crowned with a cupola of green lattice work, making it appear like an amateur picture in water-colors. Here we stop but ten minutes, and a boy comes with a box of tarantula nests for the edification of tourists. These nests are sold for fifty cents a piece, and are indeed a curiosity. They are constructed in a hole in the ground, upon the sunny side of some barren hill in a mountain range. These perforations occur as frequently as holes in a pepper-box cover. The nest is composed of adobe soil, being about four inches in length and one in diameter, the outer wall of the little house having a winding crease like a miniature tower of Babel. The entrance to the nest is a kind of trap-door with hinges, and a way to fasten it on the inside. A little dot marks the place for the latch-string, so that the tarantula need not go blundering around to find the key-hole. The inside of this wonderful structure is lined with a beautiful material unknown to the world of commerce, but resembling the short delicate fur of the white mouse. The tarantula himself is an ugly looking creature, notwithstanding his architectural ingenuity. He belongs to the spider family, in fact is a kind of grandfather spider. His body is as large as a robin's egg, some are larger, with legs and arms to correspond, and short black hair, standing upright all over both body and legs.

This creature makes a web like other spiders, or may be contracts with a smaller specimen of the spider race to weave for him, as each nest has a covering like mosquito bar veil, or wire door, to prevent foreign substances from falling into the top of his nest, which stands slantwise upon the side-hill. This web is made large enough to admit the creature at the sides without tearing it, and may serve the double purpose of a net to ensnare flies for food. The tarantula likes a warm climate; in comfortable cool weather he is seldom seen upon the promenade, spending most of his time in his study. When tourists desire to see one, they take a pitcher of cold water and pour it through the net-work at the opening, and the pompous looking creature will appear as promptly as some corpulent old gentleman who had been disturbed by the rudeness of malicious little boys jerking the door-bell while he was taking his after-dinner nap. The tarantula is no coward, but with his fussy motion, demands an explanation as much as if he were an injured individual and could speak. These creatures are frequently called from their retreats, lured into an open mouth bottle and preserved in alcohol as a curiosity. Fighting tarantulas is quite a pastime with some tourists; two or three of them are placed in close quarters and they will bite one another until both die of poison. The gratification of this amusement lies in the fact that they destroy each other. For a general thing their bite is little more thought of than the sting of a wasp, but persons in this State have been poisoned to death by their venom.

Whisky is the antidote ; perhaps this is the reason that its bite is not feared much by the residents, a large proportion of the population being in a perpetual state to resist the bite of spiders or reptiles. We leave Coulterville thinking it a pretty quiet place; nice as a resort for invalids needing a change of air. As we ascend the mountains we catch views of snow capped peaks and occasionally see rocks near at hand, having such a mixture of white quartz, that we are led to think that they are patches of snow also. As night approaches, the mountains in the distance suggest to the imagination the far off promised land. The sun sinking upon the snow clad peaks, the tinted clouds, the mysterious points and depressions may pass for the spires and domes of our Father's house where there are many mansions. As old Sol sinks to rest the whole scene becomes so glorified one can easily imagine the unfolding of the pearly gates of Paradise; still, a purple atmosphere veils this better land, covering it with mystery that hope sighs to penetrate, and this keeps urging on. In a certain altitude, the pretty manzanita shrub appears with its smooth brown bark and rich foliage. The fruit, a berry about the size of large pea and shaped exactly like an apple, is often called the manzanita apple. The vegetation is much the same upon this route as upon that of the Mariposa. The same growth appearing at certain altitudes. The first night out we stop at a place called Dudley's Mills, an oasis in the rugged mountain, abounding in fruitful greenness, a little haven given for the rest of weary tourists. It was some such place where Bunyan's Christian Pilgrim rested and in his sleep let fall his diploma, and when he awoke refreshed became so infatuated with the premises that he wandered off forgetting his roll, leaving it lying in the bower where he rested. Now a tourist would be in a similar dilema if he should fall asleep at Dudley's and loose his ticket to the Yosemite Valley, and after leaving the next morning when the grass was sparkling with dew, be obliged to retrace his steps at noonday, and wait for the next tri-weekly stage; he would then be just in the right frame of mind to sympathize with Bunyan's Christian Pilgrim, poor fellow. Upon the Coulterville route we get the very best specimens of California hotel keeping. The food is the best possible quality, prepared and served by an intelligent housewife; no better recommendation needed. The hotels throughout this State generally, are an abomination; only to be tolerated from the most extreme necessity. I do not know of another business fraud so systematized, unless it is the liquor business, for all liquors are tampered with until only fit for just what they are doing, killing men.

It is a subject of much regret among the traveling public, that the question of the quality of food served to the unfortunate traveler cannot be made a matter of special legislation. A race of men must deteriorate when fed upon refuse food, only fit for swine. I sincerely believe that this method of cooking is half the cause of there being so much intemperance in this State. I know that the old Washingtonians used to blame *women* who were poor or careless cooks, for the drunkenness of their husbands, and I think the responsibility can with safety be shifted upon the hotels in this case. A returning foreign tourist stopping for the night at Dudley's, found that in making change he had taken five or six one cent pieces for the gold coin two dollars and fifty cents. I comforted him by saying that I was ashamed of some classes of my countrymen, those who would resort to such shabbiness ; that he must educate his eyes to the specie and look sharp for one cent upon every piece in the future. The gentleman appeared to be a man of means, as he did not lay it to heart very heavily, only looked thoughtful as if trying to reconnoiter memory in order if possible to recollect when and by whom this fraud could have been practiced so successfully.

The fields at Dudley's are irrigated, and the **birds** have found that it is a beautiful home in the forest for them, and they make it lively with their music. During our forenoon ride we came to the Bower Cave; this is situated but a short distance from the main road, and is visited while the horses drink. A young girl conducted us to the cave and opened a rude door fastened by lock and key. We descended a flight of stairs long enough for two stories of an ordinary residence, and find ourselves in an amphitheater of most wonderful pleasing appearance; being one hundred feet long and seventy-five feet wide. The walls formed of great rocky bowlders coming nearly together at the top, and three large trees, three and a half feet in diameter, growing in the cave, just a nice distance apart, the boughs coming together at the top, forming a complete shade like green blinds to a sky light, and softening the light in consequence. The floor of the cave is smooth hard soil, ornamented with little patches of green moss, answering as rugs placed about upon bare floors. Upon one side of the cave is a pond of water, occupying not more than one-fourth or one-fifth of the space. This water is deep, clear as crystal, very cold and having a perpendicular wall of two feet, as it is two feet lower than the floor of the cave; it is enclosed with a paling to prevent accident, and a small boat is furnished for fishing purposes, as it abounds in these beautiful mountain trout. At one end of the pond nature has attempted to form a stairway leading to the galleries. The arches overhead are complete, and the natural way may have answered for the original design, but the stairs have been finished by the hand of man, and we ascend to pass through a spacious hall to dark side rooms twenty feet deep, and many other black holes we did not care to penetrate. These places have all been visited, perhaps by wild beasts, as the openings were worn as if by something sliding upon them.

I was enjoying, and wondering if nature fitted up these mansions on purpose for her dusky sons and daughters, and why such houses did not occur oftener, and where some poor homeless, houseless wanderers could have the benefit, instead of taking up with the terrible hotels in this State; and when I aroused from these reveries, found myself alone with the little lady guide; all the tourists had fled and when we reached the top of the steps there was not one in sight. This is an objection to traveling with a public conveyance for pleasure or culture. Most persons visiting those places, go for the simple sake of going, without the least idea of ever becoming cultivated in scenery or intelligently benefitted by travel. When I reached the road, the stages were waiting, the drivers with uplifted lash ready to be off, as if our lives depended upon getting out of this vicinity with all possible speed. I was astonished, at the same time provoked, to hear the comments of tourists upon this beautiful curiosity. All would say at least, that it was nice; some were annoyed at being charged fifty cents upon our return, others that the stage had lost that much time, and some that the path over which we went was so rough with stones. Verily, man is a grumbling animal; it is almost a wonder that he ever learned to articulate in a perfect language, when growling might have served his purpose quite as well. To an educated cavern tourist, I suppose that this cave would be a very small thing, but to me who have never visited many caves, it is wonderful and beautiful, and I shall hereafter make a point of visiting all caves anywhere within the range of my travels. This day at noon we stop at a place called Hazel Green. We find an excellent lunch house, kept during summer by James Halstead, a very pleasant and obliging host. In this remote mountain forest, we pay one dollar for lunch and think it not one cent too much for value received.

Leaving this point we descend the mountain until we reach the Yosemite. The horses pass rapidly around these mountain curves, bringing new scenes and fresh pictures in every turn; many water falls appear which lend a charming variety to the scene, although considered too insignificant to have a name when compared to the legitimate falls of the real Yosemite. As we near the end of the second day from Merced, the third from San Francisco, we hear the roar of the rushing Merced river, and soon find ourselves on an elevation of about three or four thousand feet above a yawning precipice, and looking timidly down, down, to get a glimpse of a beautiful stream of the most delicate shade of green when placid, and white as snow when broken into dancing cascades by rocky obstructions. At this point the great Yosemite Valley first breaks upon the vision, with a realizing sense of its grandeur. Here the rocks lift their towering heads so loftily to the sky, and the precipices are so fearfully deep, that mighty streams all turn to tears when rushing by, because of taking such a leap. The great mass of clean, clearly cut bowlders lying along the wall of the valley, broken by their fall into all conceivable shapes, resembling a fleet of steam ships driven by the storm upon some rocky strand in the greatest possible confusion. Much of this stone is the same as the celebrated Lockport granite. The figures varying with clouds of black running through the light colored granite, some spotted in large patterns, and some figured almost like print. These are frequently called the calico rocks, and if accessible would make the most beautiful and substantial building material in the world. The road is blasted through this rocky *débris* and it takes the most watchful diligence to keep the thoroughfare clear from obstructions.

WHAT I SAW AND HEARD IN THE VALLEY.

UPON entering Yosemite Valley it is quite natural to think about how this wonderful formation was wrought out. I came to the conclusion that the top of a range of mountains about fifteen miles long and two or three in width had fallen in, to fill some subterraneous vacuum. The fact that there is so little *débris* upon the ground shows that all the matter was taken down at one slide, leaving walls fearfully perpendicular, four thousand feet high upon an average. Then in all probability the valley filled with water, and was the cause of these bottomless little lakes we hear of among the mountains. The soil is very like beach sand — heavy and coarse — making locomotion exceedingly difficult for both man and beast. There are other evidences in this valley of its having been once the bed of a lake. Upon reading Professor Whitney's work upon the Yosemite and Sierras, I find that his theories and suppositions are the same. Waterfalls are formed frequently throughout the valley by the melting snows running in rivulets, seeking one common outlet; and the beautiful Merced winds its way upon one side and the other of the enclosure, as if to impartially dispense its liquid blessings and accommodate itself to the rocky obstruction and sympathizing waterfall. It will be delightful when rustic bridges have been built across these twinkling, pebbly tributaries. The whole valley is densely shaded (except now and then small openings) with the variety of timber growing in this altitude — the pines, spruce, cedar, and balm of Gilead or cottonwood — the growth of underwood consisting of manzanita, dogwood and the usual mountain chaparral. The fragrant azalea, the thimble berry and spicy colt's foot form the first covering for the soil. The pines are models of perfection, and would make as fine lumber as any timber upon earth. I suppose it will shock lovers of scenery, and sound sacrelegious, to hear these park-like forests and grand old trees mentioned in a practical sense. This place should be looked upon as sacred, being a glorious old curiosity shop, donated by the General Government and adopted by the State as a ward for the benefit and cultivation of the traveling public through all coming time.

A person cannot appreciate the magnitude of these walls without lingering near them for some time, and then they must be carefully, studiously compared with all the pinnacles and elevations one has ever climbed. I remember to have thought a hundred and seven feet pretty well up from the ground, when climbing to the tower of a village water tank; but to compare this height with three or four thousand feet perpendicular is rather more than one can comprehend with the eye when it comes to altitude. These walls so overshadow things that the valley seems the coolest, quietest place of resort in all the world. Distance is obscured by the height of the surroundings. If one attempts to walk to an object apparently close at hand, he will be astonished at the space annihilated before the point is gained. Glacier Point gives the finest view to be obtained in the whole valley. An entire day will be consumed in reaching it, but it is well worth the time and pains. From this height — four thousand feet — Mirror Lake is seen to reflect the surrounding mountains as plainly as a looking-glass will reflect the human form. All the principle points of interest can be seen from this place, and the immense height fills one with awe and a kind of delightful terror.

After reaching the valley, the next thing is to look for a place where one is to breakfast, have lunch put up, dine and sleep after the day's labor is over, for nothing in this world is worth having for which we do not work, and the Yosemite trip is no exception to this rule. Lidig's is the best place in the line of hotels. Mrs. L. attends to the cooking in person; the results are that the food is well cooked and intelligently served. There is not the variety to be obtained here as in places more accessible to market. After traveling a few months in California a person is liable to think less of variety and more of quality. At this place the beds are cleanly and wholesome, although consisting of pulu mattresses placed upon slat bedsteads. This house stands in the shadow of Sentinel Rock, and faces the great Yosemite Fall; is surrounded with porches, making a pleasant place to sit and contemplate the magnificence of the commanding scenery. At this place there are several beautiful but sadly neglected children, who act as a kind of scare-crow — frightening tourists off to some other parts, who repent upon learning the real nature of the place, beholding the spotless floors, and the actual purity of the linen and things in general.

The horses used by the tourist upon the trail form a peculiar feature in the business of Yosemite life. After a day's work these creatures are dismounted at any of the hotels and turned loose. They proceed at once, without telling, to the stables adjoining and a large corral. where they are unsaddled; then they trot off a mile or two, perhaps three, to a pasture, to rest and feed for the coming day's labor, always in droves of from a dozen to fifty. The next morning the guides hunt them, and they are driven up like a drove of cattle, some one of the number wearing a disgraceful old cow bell. They tramp to the stables like sheep to slaughter, are placed in the corral, taken out and saddled in squads, as they are needed, sometimes standing for hours waiting the pleasure of creation's lord. These horses are treated like slaves, having neither time nor opportunity to get sufficient food or rest to fully recuperate them from the previous day's exertions. The consequences are that they are as spiritless as so many sheep. These creatures are raised in droves upon the San Joaquin plains, all bearing the brand of the owner. I was horrified to learn that when the mothers are needed for work the colts are given away or knocked in the head. Horses are reared in this climate with so little trouble and expense, that strangers are astonished at the cheapness with which they are held. Good serviceable creatures can be had all the way from fifty cents to fifty dollars. The companies owning the horses in the valley have a kind of asylum for them, where they are permitted to retire when too much exhausted to continue upon the trail. Here in this green meadow some of them recuperate, and some take a journey to the better land, where it is to be hoped that men will not desire to enrich themselves at the expense of the animal comfort of any of God's creatures. Somehow in my heart I cannot but feel that the man or class of men who will totally disregard the common wants and the dignity of any animal will hardly manifest the purest humanity and manhood toward his own kind.

There are several hotels in the Yosemite Valley, a bath house, picture gallery, a place where the curiosities in wood work are to be obtained, a seed store, dry goods store, laundry and meat market. There is at present no resident physician, but likely there will be those who will at least take up a temporary abode by the time of another season for tourists. The bath house called the Cosmopolitan is kept by John C. Smith, and I will venture to say that there is nothing in this line in the State that is as well gotten up or as well kept. I wish there were more of the same race of John Smiths to take charge of a few of the hotels in this country.

The Great Register is found here, a book something like the one described by John the Revelator, which had so many seals — this having the names of the different States, whereof the inhabitants upon visiting the Yosemite can register thereof. In this establishment there are reading rooms, billiard tables, croquet grounds — amusement for both sexes — and walks with flowers kept with the utmost care and scrupulous neatness. Near this elegant establishment is the house of Adolph Sinning, a skillful worker in wood. Mr. Sinning has made a chess table of two dozen different kinds of wood and two thousand pieces. This beautiful piece of workmanship was on exhibition at the city of Philadelphia during the Centennial. Pretty little cabinets, canes and sleeve buttons are manufactured from the timber grown in Yosemite Valley. This gentleman is a German, of most pleasing presence and manner, and does all this fine work entirely alone. He says that as a mechanic he has great respect for the American, and a due regard for his modes of procedure; but that the American rushes things so terribly that he cannot work with him, and can only succeed by doing things in his own quiet way. He showed me a cane with a setting of stone or glass in the side a little larger than a pin head. Upon placing this to the eye a beautiful stereoscopic view of the Yosemite Fall spread out before the astonished gaze.

There is a seed store kept next door by Henry Segman, where the seed of the *Sequoys Gigantus,* or Big Tree, is kept for sale, aside from many other kinds of vegetable growths to be found in the valley. The big trees flourish finely in any of the snowy latitudes where the frost is not too severe. In England it is said that they shoot up two feet in one season, having a very vigorous growth. The oily seed of the balsam of fir is collected in considerable quantities, and sold for six dollars per pound. The picture gallery is kept by J. J. Rieley. I found an ugly looking lot of samples hanging in frames about the valley, and when I saw his real pictures inquired how it was that such bad samples were put out for an advertisement. He said that the good pictures would all be stolen as fast as he could replace them. I wondered at the cupidity of any one coming here who would steal a picture, let it be ever so tempting, when they could be obtained at the price of twenty-five and fifty cents. There is a post and telegraph office and Wells & Fargo's express. The people one sees and hears in these watering places form a goodly feature in the objects of travel. At present the hotels of the Yosemite are of bandbox order — cloth and paper, to be sure, answering all the immediate needs of this indulgent climate, but rather generous in the communication of sound. My first morning dreams were disturbed by the wail of some venerable spinster who had lost her wash-rag. The chambermaid was rallied at five o'clock in the morning, and the din and search kept up with unceasing diligence for one hour. During this time I had heard the word wash-rag pronounced so frequently, that this, with the fatigue of travel, threw me into a laughing hysteric. There was something so utterly ridiculous in hearing the word pronounced so repeatedly, and the absurdity of creating a disturbance for so small a matter, that I came near having what

THE GREAT YOSEMITE FALLS.

used to be known as a "conniption" fit. In the meantime the poor little chambermaid was vibrating between smiles and tears mentally, and between my room, the other room and the porch personally, all the time wondering what could have become of the unfortunate woman's wash-rag. The smiles were in sympathy with my laughing mood, the tears the cruel sting of unjust accusation, and the bodily movements an uneasy desire to have the stage come and carry off the hapless tourist. The stage came at last, and the woman was torn from the scenes where she had lost her wash-rag and borne reluctantly away. The last sound that I heard from her retreating figure-head was the wail of the wash-rag. In the course of her morning work the chambermaid went into the room, and upon emptying the pitcher gave a faint scream, and called me to come and behold the missing wash-rag. "Stars and stripes!" I exclaimed, "where did you find it?" "In the pitcher," she answered. It was a piece of tufted toweling about a foot square, and striped with red, and when it came sliding out of the pitcher the girl imagined pink snakes, curiosities of tourists, and several things before the real truth flashed upon her. This mystery was solved: "but," said the girl, "I know that lady will think until the day of judgment that I took her wash-rag, unless by some accident she shall hear of this." I lost a package of thread, of spools of cotton and silk, upon this same route — not at this house — enough to have lasted me for ten years; and I am sure that with a warrant I could find them now, but I would rather lose them than run the risk of placing an innocent person under unjust suspicion; besides, there are classes of human beings whose chances to compete with others for a livelihood have been so cramped and limited, that they think that they must steal in order to get even, and it is not in my heart to blame them. At the same time I would most assuredly encourage the most rigorous regard for the property of others, as stealing is closely allied to the dreadful crime of murder.

One morning I heard a young girl say, in a whining voice, that she did not want to make the trip on horseback necessary to do the valley, adding that she did not see what people wanted to go scrambling over those rough trails for. I am afraid; should think people could come here and enjoy this beautiful scenery in quiet. But papa had a horse brought, and insisted with a few firm but gentle words, as if accustomed to being obeyed; and every evening when this dainty little miss returned, face flushed with exercise, and so stiff from sitting upon the horse that she could scarcely step, she would call out to those whom she greeted at the hotel, "O, I am so glad that I went; it was so beautiful!" Papa evidently had no idea of going to the trouble and expense of bringing her to this valley, have her lose her interest, and go tamely home without seeing anything. Upon another occasion a very pretty, well dressed family came for a few days, and the wife seemed to be parsimonious. Each morning she had something to say about the extravagance of the trip. The husband would answer, It is a pity, with such an income, that we cannot spend a little money in traveling without such a to do. I do not want to hear another word; not another word. This seemed to settle the matter for another day. But they were a very unhappy couple, in spite of their income; and the children seemed to catch the same spirit — were constantly teasing one another and quarreling.

When you visit the Yosemite for pleasure and put up at a pasteboard hotel, bring as few cares and family jars as you can well get along with, and above all keep quiet while remaining. Contrasting this scene, there was a middle aged, corpulent man with an immense wide mouth, heavy chin and narrow forehead. The individual evidently had a daughter with him, the perfact counterpart of the governor, as the boys would say, and in their party were two or three empty headed fops seeking the old man's favor by the way of the daughter's moneyed prospects. The old gentleman condescendingly took it upon himself to entertain the younger members of the party by relating stale stories in the most pompous manner, sometimes getting the point on the wrong end of the anecdote, while the chaps made their own points likely by laughing in a very appreciative manner, perhaps at the old fellow's obtuseness and lack of intellectual tact. At any rate the scene was really interesting as a characteristic, even to those not at all in the plot. The anxious mamma is a character one meets in all of these places of public resort. She is known by the manner in which she hurls sharpened darts at any interesting female who should happen to stand in the shadow of the young or old man that she has chosen to marry her Serephena Ann. Now, I detest, above all the characters that I ever met, the anxious mamma; and there is nothing which man can say that will so insult my womanhood as to hear him, in his vanity, gloat over the traps and snares of this class of female slaves; slaves to the absurd customs of what is known as society. I know that I would never become an ambitious mamma. If I had twenty-seven daughters. and their orders of intelligence varied from the finest first-class literary talents down to that of the second-class scrub, I would fit them for lives of usefulness to themselves and to society; and teach them that marriage should be the last subject upon earth upon which to spend time and thought, even though it be the first thing perpetrated. Men do not appreciate women that they can pick up like pebbles upon the strand, nor do they deserve any more than they get in the way of appreciation, because of their want of independence and dignity.

On account of the crowded state of the hotel a couple of gentlemen were obliged to room together, hitherto strangers to one another. One was a German-American, of good practical sense but bad English, while the other was, I think, an Englishman. The following dialogue occurred while they were preparing a toilet for breakfast:

Englishman. "Well, a gentleman is a gentleman the world over, and I have no objections to rooming with a gentleman. I do not care if you are a German duke or general, I should have no objection."

German. "My Got, man! I am just as goot as any duke or general, and I earned my own money, and do not thank Got, man nor the other member of the trinity."

E. "My house was founded in the time of

Queen Elizabeth (here the conversation became inaudible).

The hotels were in a very crowded state, and men of any rank took what was offered them. This was better, somewhat, than taking a blanket and lying under a tree for a night's rest.

I wondered if I could detect this scion of nobility at the breatfast table. I looked down the rows on each side: sure enough he was there. A careful observer could have picked him out from among ten or twenty men of sense, either of whom could have traced their ancestry to the hold of an imigrant ship, and their line to a tarred mark upon the deck better appreciated by our forefathers than by ourselves. I knew him by his handsome feminine face and brainless cranium; by the style of his neck-tie, shirt-front and the number and size of his finger rings; and most of all by his condescending good nature and patronizing smile. Living relic of degenerate greatness, thought I, quoting Pope:

> "Go, if your ancient but ignoble blood
> Has crept through ninnies ever since the flood.
> Go, and pretend your family is young,
> Nor own your fathers have been fools so long."

Many celebrities and what might be termed "characters" come to this valley every season. No "roughs," however, have as yet made a rendezvous of this earthly paradise. Here I met Sallie Hart, the well known female teacher's lobbiest, of this State; a golden haired " childy " little woman, but one of acknowledged talent and much political influence, backed in all her public movements by the wealth and talent of the suffragists and temperance people of this State. Also, Mrs. Lawrence, a conservative but graceful writer, who is known by the unpretending *nom de plume*, " Red Riding Hood."

I would like a few words to ministers and their families who come to visit this wonder in nature. That in these days of Christian popularity and church prosperity, few are called upon to practice much self-denial at home, and when in this valley it is an excellent time to exercise the Christian graces; and if the beds are not so soft as those you have been accustomed to, just thing of the hymn, " Shall I be carried to the skies on flowery beds of ease," etc., and if you are called upon to eat grass-hoppers and fresh bread, think of an apostle whose meat was locusts and wild honey; and that the beloved founder of Christianity had not a better place to lay his holy head than under the grateful shade of these lofty pines in the Yosemite Valley; and it is very doubtful if the ass which he appropriated was any more spirited than the poor beasts which bore us so laboriously over the rough mountain trail, bearing the brand of **Washburn, Chapman & Co.**

STRAWBERRYING IN THE YOSEMITE VALLEY.

A PARTY of three were going for a drive towards the upper end of this enchanting valley, and as if to tempt the fates, who are said to be partial to odd numbers, I was invited to fill a vacant seat and make the number even. The horses were of the sedate, thoughtful type, born to take things complacently, and without any fiery or spirited nonsense about them, and when encouraged by the lash, invariably expressing the same start of surprise, immediately settling into their original gait, as if they believed the driver's suggestions to be purely accidental. The driver represented among men what the team did among horses. He was a descendant of the noble Castilian, subject to the modification of the various crosses which have taken place in the peculiar commingling of races upon the Pacific coast. Our driver might have prided himself upon speaking four or five different languages, without being able to read in either, and in each of these dialects his vocabulary may have been so limited that it would be quite impossible to elicit an intelligent response to the most common-place inquiry. From constitutional peculiarities, our driver's virtues must ever be his greatest faults, a paradox, but nevertheless applying with equal truth to both men and horses. At the first outset the wagon squeaked so fearfully that we were afraid our voices could not be heard—a very uncomfortable state of things for an excessively talkative party. The gentleman of the company, Captain B., a Massachusetts Yankee, proposed to the driver that we put into some harbor a sufficient length of time to grease the wheels, remarking that the hubs might heat, and that this might interfere with our locomotion. It was evident that the Captain knew more of ship rigging than he did of horses and their fixtures, for a single glance at those natural born scrubs would have convinced any one but a seaman that the hubs were not in as much danger of heat by friction as we were of sunstroke by stagnation. The boy of doubtful nationality and mixed dialects, was sufficiently Americanized to pay no attention to the Captain's suggestions, and soon the noisy wheels were forgotten in contemplating the grandeur of the walls of this mighty tabernacle. The air was pure and bracing, the vegetation lending a delightful fragrance, and the party were filled with wonder which was vented in exclamations. These gigantic walls so overshadow things as to make the valley appear much smaller than it really is. After a delightful drive of two hours we reach the end of the wagon road, and return on a diverging route in order to come near the Yosemite Falls. In our course lies the transparent Merced, spanned by a bridge of most remarkable architectural structure. Two logs, or stringers, are laid across the stream and floored with planks, which are fastened down with wooden pins. At present it is so much settled upon one side as to leave in fearful doubt the center of gravity of a passing vehicle.

There is a ford that can be crossed with some risk at this season of the year, as the water is yet rather high and so limpid that one is liable to be deceived in the depth. Being upon the front seat beside the driver I took the liberty to suggest that fording might be better than flying in our present ill-fledged condition, that this was a promising bridge, but that the promise was entirely too one-sided. My argument prevailed, perhaps appealed to the judgment of the driver. The horses plunged into the stream like lazy porpoises, apparently delighted with the prospect of swimming, commencing to drink as they waded, going slower and slower, as the water became deeper. The dull creatures took it so leisurly, and with such a relish, that I should have been more alarmed than surprised if they had attempted to lie down and roll over. The water already came so high that my hair stood on end. I had drawn several drowning sighs and the crisis was not yet reached, but in another moment the water came pouring over the little dash-board. I gave a faint, feminine shriek, elevated my feet upon a level with the seat, the driver hit the horses, they gave a start, and the trouble was over. We had crossed; not entirely dry shod, for the Captain and his wife did not see the situation in time to save their soles from the impending fate. During this adventure I was fearfully exercised mentally, making a vigorous resolve to devote the remainder of my efforts upon earth to suppress any disposition towards officiousness. However the peril was passed and soon forgotten; and it is surprising how rapidly clothing dries in this clear evaporating atmosphere. Shortly after we find ourselves in a circular piece of meadow land surrounded by a growth of fine young trees. This is the land of wild strawberries, where I was tempted to go a-berrying to recall the days of youth, and to pay very dear for the whistle. Directly in front of us was that white-robed spirit, known as the Yosemite Falls, descending like a million sky rockets over two thousand feet of fall to baptize the rocks below and gladden the fertile valleys. Occasionally its snowy drapery is blown aside by the busy breeze, returning gracefully like a hanging curtain.

This beautiful piece of natural scenery engenders veneration and sublimity in the human mind. I found myself changing a passage in Goldsmith's Deserted Village to suit the occasion:

> In all my wanderings around this world of care,
> In all my griefs, and God has given my share,
> I still had hope some pleasant hours to crown,
> Besides these grand old rocks to sit me down,
> To draw an inspiration from these scenes to last
> Until the latest hour of life is past.

In driving through the meadow I observed a plat of wild strawberries. If I stopped to pick them then there was nothing to put them in, so we passed on. Bright visions of rose-tinted, hopeful youth flitted through my brain. I could not be content without returning to this field and getting a few strawberries, just to refresh my memory upon the days of pink sunbonnets and Old Lang Syne. The next morning I procured a four quart pail and started for the red field of action. A road never seemed so long. It was reported a mile and a half, but I am sure that it was three miles. Once started I must reach the ground, and reaching it must procure some of the wild fruit, and then walk back unless a miracle interposed to save the infliction. Upon reaching the slanting bridge, I ventured across on foot, and on doing so modified my mental resolution in regard to officiousness, for I now began to think that my interposition the day before saved us from being tipped into the cool Merced. I never in my life felt more keenly that I had been deceived in distance, but comforted myself by saying that three miles is no distance for a British subject to walk. I had become very warm, tired and thirsty; the Merced flowed nearly around the meadow, and before I commenced my picking, dipped my pail into the river and drank of the refreshing water. I envy the cattle that can quench their thirst at this stream the year round. It is the coolest, sweetest tasting water that I ever drank, and is as soft as snow-water—just what it is. It comes near to the Bartlett Spring in flavor. I gathered a quart of berries, went to the river, wet my handkerchief, placed it in my hat and started for home, (we sometimes call the hotels in this country by that name.) This field did not seem wide, still

I observed horsemen upon the other side and they looked as if they were in an adjoining county. I wandered along, occasionally stopping at a red patch, and this fascination continued to hold me until I had added three quarts to my gatherings; by this time the edge of the field was reached. I was thirsty again and wondered how I could ever have started off on such a journey without a lunch and cup to drink from. This was verily much like the heedlessness of youth. But I was perishing with thirst and my pail was in use. There was no other way but to build a pier of drift-wood and drink hunter fashion. This was performed with some labor; then I steered for the meadow and was on the road for home, feeling a little as if youthful pastimes were a humbug. I should have felt more decided in regard to these reflections if I could conscientiously say that age always brought wisdom. I am firmly convinced that it does not, for I still find myself controlled at times by strange freaks that would tend to question the common sense of a child ten years of age. At length the hotel was reached and an elderly lady offered to help me hull my berries. This task completed I went to the kitchen and gave orders as to how the berries were to be divided among my acquaintances. The stages came in before dinner and there was a rush of hungry passengers. I put in a claim that I had been without eating for ten hours and had been a-berrying. My claim was granted, and in the course of table serving I had a dish of the wild strawberries. Upon going to my room I found myself getting fearfully sea-sick without a thought of going to sea. Soon I had lost all my berries and supper too. The system was exhausted and the stomach promptly resented any further imposition in the way of work. The next two days I was unable to sit up. It took twenty-four hours for my acquaintances to realize that I was ill, and when they called I inquired if they had received any of the wild berries. Not one, they answered. The servants were rushed out of their senses and no one knew anything about them. I was overwhelmed with disappointment; how should I get even? upon whom could I be revenged? If I were a male member of society, a privileged citizen, could have vented my rage and ire in kicks, cuffs and forcible language, but being a restricted nondescript with many asserted liberties and little practical freedom, I restrained my feelings, took a pill of asafœtida and found my temper becoming calm. I perhaps could have had the satisfaction of kicking over a chair, but the muscles brought into use upon the strawberry field refused to act in concert with healthy locomotion. If any person had at that time called me a failure or an unmitigated humbug, I should have believed the statement. While lying in bed I had time to reflect upon the uncertainty of human affairs, and realize, in the language of the Widow Bedott:

> We can't calculate with no precision,
>   On naught beneath the sky,
> So I have come to the decision
>   That 'taint no use to try.

Owing to the transient character of the Yosemite travel, in getting about after two days illness, all my acquaintances were gone and their places filled with strangers. Like Rip Van

Winkle, I was led to exclaim, I knew who were my neighbors when I went to sleep. I had lost three days of active life and one sleeve button. The strawberries, even those eaten were a total loss — mine going to the dogs, and the rest devoured by non-sympathizing tourists. Here, in sight of the beautiful Yosemite Falls, I came to the conclusion that we have no more right to sigh over our youthful days than we have to covet our neighbor's horses or his overcoat. That the roses of youth are so entwined with verdancy that we gain more than we lose by our transit into the sear and yellow leaf. That no one period of human life possesses an advantage over another, and I resolve to accept the laws of compensation, let by-gones be by-gones, and remember no more the days nor the follies of youth.

VERNAL AND NEVADA FALLS.

THESE interesting falls are reached from the valley by a zigzag trail which can only be traversed on foot, or upon animals. We started at nine o'clock in the morning the guide going ahead in order to point out and call the names of places of interest. The ride through any part of the timber is most delightful, being as shady as one continued park. The weather is just cool enough, just warm enough, in short it seems made for the special comfort of tourists and if the winds are tempered to the shorn lamb, why should not the goats come in for a share of this temperature? We meander slowly through pleasant glades, glens, and intervals, crossing mountain streams, beautifully speckled with pieces of pulverized granite, worn until they take the name pebble, rivulets possessing so much of picturesque beauty, that it hardly seems possible for them to exist outside of poetical imagination. Here are the stately pine and red wood, the graceful, although illegitimate cedar, the beautiful silver fir, also the balm of Gilead. The showy dog wood displays its gay blosoms, the spicy plant known as colt's foot grows luxuriantly in this altitude, the fair azalea decorates the open glade and lends its aroma to the passing breeze. The animals, poor creatures, are over worked and not properly fed, hence the most spiritless, sheepish looking creatures one can imagine; they pass demurely along in single file ever slow and cautious. As we begin to ascend the mountain, the trail becomes rougher and it is wonderful the rock's hard-heads, rolling stones and other obstructions these patient creatures will overcome. After an hour's cool pleasant riding, the sound of rushing water breaks upon our ears, increasing in roar until conversation becomes impossible, and the clear Merced, in a different course, comes dashing, tearing, roaring down o'er the mountain we are climbing. It pours, rushes with terrible force over mighty rocks and helpless drift-wood, sometimes appearing like a flock of wolf-hunted sheep, then broken into snowy fleeces and here and there running into great clear streams of liquid green, ever in fearful tearing haste to join the placid river flowing calmly through the quiet valley. The rush of these waters create a strong breeze which is wonderfully refreshing, although we are not sensible of any undue heat. We scramble up a trail harder than the way of the transgressor, and arrive at the toll house, for this road is built by private enterprise, and must be kept open and in repair at the expense of the tourists. Here we alight, tie our sheep-like steeds, pay a toll of seventy-five cents, and scramble over the rocks on foot, including a vigorous use of hands, in order to get a better view of the Vernal Falls. At length we reach a large flat stone that might with much appropriateness be called table rock. This is covered with a plat of green moss, and seems as if fixed for the purpose of giving a fine view of this fall, notwithstanding one's literal hard scramble to reach it. This sheet of water descends over the walls of this mighty fortification three hundred and fifty feet. Of course, streams passing into the valley naturally seek the lowest and most accessible part of the wall in its immediate vicinity. The voice of this cataract reaches one's ears long before its snowy presence greets the vision, breaking the grand majestic panorama of ever varying rocks. This fall has a breath as well as a voice. After receiving our misty baptism from nature's flowing font, I sing "Nearer my God to thee, nearer to thee." What though it be a Fall that bringeth me.

We then scrambled back to the toll house, a building about twenty feet long and fourteen in width, and located under the edge of a speckled granite rock of the steamboat shape, the stone forming the back part of the house and half of the roof, giving it a cave like appearance. There are many bowlders of this peculiar shape. There is one located near the trail known as the steamboat rock. The form is large and flat upon the top like the deck of a steamer, and runs in upon two sides, making the bottom smaller, giving it the appearance of a ship upon the dry docks; and seem to have been floated and left high and dry, or have run aground in some of nature's volcanic freaks. Some of them have springs of water forming a little pond in which they seem to rest content, rather than to shrink and shed their mossy barnacles from very dryness.

This rocky formation is really one of the wonders of the valley, and is in reality bowlders which have been cleaved out of the stupendous walls when shaken by earthquakes, and when they have fallen, the large flat surface downward, do not attract the attention of the observer, because resembling nothing upon the earth, but when lying the small end downward, the resemblance is too much like a steamship to be overlooked. The toll house was grafted upon this singular formation, lessening the expense one-half, roof and all. There is yet room for a livery stable and necessary out buildings under the protecting wing of the same mighty bowlder. Again we mount our sheepish steeds and commence the ascent of a zigzag trail, our winding way upward over hanging precipices of fearful height and depth. The animals, both horses and mules, show a peculiar individuality not observed heretofore in their sleepy manners. They assert themselves as much as to say, "We understand this trail, and the business of this ascent must be left to us entirely. We know just where you are going, and that we are responsible for both our lives, and must therefore be allowed to proceed without dictation." Hence, they halt at every turn to take breath, stopping and starting when they please. They seem to ignore the interference of man, both as to what they can endure, and the choice of picking their own foothold. One soon learns to repose perfect confidence in the careful creatures, ceases to tug at the reins when he finds it of no avail, and anxiously trusts to the fates for daring to tempt providence. Soon the greatest anxiety comes from the fact that the animal moves so slowly that there is danger of his falling asleep and forgetting to move altogether. My poor, dear beast when stopping for breath, would turn his head, lay back his ears and look out upon the tops of the forest trees and down the precipice as if he did not think much of this style of scenery. Sometimes he had sufficient spirit to snort when turning his eyes thoughtfully back upon the rocky trail.

At length we reach a certain point, not the summit but the climax of our expectations, and commence a descent upon the other side. Presently the Nevada Falls comes in sight, the cap of Liberty, and Mount Washington and Mount Broderick. Nevada Fall rushes over a precipice seven hundred feet high, and in width is much like the spiritual looking Yosemite Fall. It appears to be about four feet in width, while the Vernal seems to be ten or twenty. These tall, or long cataracts, all descend in the form of sky rockets, while the shorter cascades are more compact, forming a solid, moving, white sheet. Nevada Fall sends forth an atmosphere heavy with mist, and at three or four o'clock in the afternoon, rainbows may be seen with dazzling brilliancy and the primitive colors in varied shapes. The draft caused by these rushing elements, keeps a few white clouds hovering over this cataract, like guardian angels, the only clouds to be seen in the deep ether above, and the cool breath of this baptizing spirit, compelled us to retreat into our thickest wraps while standing face to face, contemplating its graceful grandeur. The Cap of Liberty, a rock standing four thousand six hundred feet above the valley, and clear from its surroundings, is, according to my fancy, the most interesting granite giant in the whole valley. It is stupendous beyond conception, and with its cap-like outlines, standing against the clear blue sky, it presents to the beholder one of the wonders of the world in magnitude. I did not feel able to stand and view my dumb stone chief from head to foot, his greatness so overwhelmed me that I sought a reclining position that I might have a place to hold my head in case my brain reeled in his majestic presence.

We have now been a half hour at Snow's, the name of the man who keeps the hotel or lunch house in this remote location, a place only known to the pleasure seeking tourist, and the few who make a business of guiding him hither. I am so fatigued from the ascent that I fall asleep upon the lounge and dream of seeing waterfalls, and hearing roaring cataracts, and wake to find my mouth dry and parched, longing for a draft from the cool Merced. I obtained it, but scarcely dare drink half a glass, because I have already drank of this water and chilled my stomach until it refuses to digest the most simple food. It seems to create an inward fever and a most unconquerable thirst. Others beside myself speak of this peculiarity of the waters, still every one is crazy to get it.

After partaking of a most excellent lunch and resting a couple of hours, we think of retracing our steps. The horses have been stabled and fed, but it would take days, weeks, months, perhaps years for them to get refreshed. Poor jaded creatures; somehow I cannot feel very tenderly toward the man who makes money by abusing other animals. I always felt an inward chuckle of delight when the guides had occasion to state that certain eccentric mules and knowing horses had so hid themselves among the rocks that they could not be found at the time they were wanted to make the laborious ascent of the trail. Somehow these creatures have my sympathy, as does every living thing that has sufficient sense to resent a wrong imposed upon it. We pay a dollar apiece for our lunch, and, because of my enfeebled digestion, I feel that I am not getting the worth of my money; therefore, desire my horse shall have my share of the meal in token of thankfulness for his care in bringing my heavy person over the precipitous road. I place a few shriveled apples in my pocket for my ragged steed. The gentlemen say that he will not eat them. I am wondering why man will continue to throw cold water upon the smallest enterprise — if that enterprise be a feminine one. Natural perversity in the disposition of the human male is wonderful in its way, and it continues to exasperate me as if it were not a thing of every day, and I might say hourly, occurence. I never get used to it; I feel as if I would like to be transmigrated into a sitting hen for the occasion, so that I might fly upon the shoulders of one of these stubborn, willful creatures and give him a good threshing with my wings, associated with a vigorous hen-pecking. But I forget that it is a woman's office to be patient, and I expect this quarrelsome disposition arises from the state of my digestion, or rather indigestion. At any rate I gave the horse the apples and he still retained enough of the Old Adam to eat it; or, according to the Darwinian theory, Adam may have retained enough of the Old Horse or Donkey to cause him to eat apples when presented by the hand of an affectionate woman. I like hopeful, believing people. Hope is a twin sister to the male Courage, and nothing of importance can ever be accomplished without both working together. I believed the horse would eat the apples, and was right; our first grand mother had the same faith, and was successful. If Adam had been looking for birds' nests to rob, and found the apple, he would not have believed that Eve cared about this variety of fruit, consequently would have eaten it himself without submitting the question or giving Eve the benefit of the doubt.

We are soon upon our horses and commence the descent, feeling well paid for the anxiety of ascending. The downward course is more difficult. The attraction of gravitation tries so hard to get the better of us that we are obliged to brace ourselves painfully against its efforts.

We go faster at any rate than we did ascending, partly because the animals are homeward bound and are anxious for their browse. We do not stop at the toll house, only glance at it and pass on. Soon we are in the valley, and so accustomed to the motion of the horses that all anxiety is dropped. The guide falls behind to gossip with that dignitary of another party, as we no longer need his services. We met a large party going up to Snow's to remain all night, and be kept awake by the musical sound of roaring cataracts. Our horses do not like to give the trail; luckily we are not upon precipitous ground; if our party had been, the others would not have been permitted to leave the toll house until we came; as it was there was little trouble and less danger; the horses crowding together and refusing to give up the trail, as if they had sole possession and did not mean to relinquish it. They persisted in placing themselves lengthwise across the track, and struggled to hold this position so that none of the other party could pass. Now comes the solid enjoyment of the trip. Beneath these grand and peaceful shades, across

BRIDAL VEIL FALL.

those picturesque pebble brooks we unconsciously scatter, each lingering carelessly behind the other, enjoying the scenes, each in own way or according to his particular fancy. The party straggled on an hour, cling to the banks of the Merced. Observing its present tranquility one would hardly believe that this was the same stream which an hour ago came madly racing with the breeze down the mountain side. At five or half past the members of the party drop unceremoniously off to their various destinations, and when I rein my steed up at the hotel steps, not one of that file of fifteen persons is present. Some were already engaged, likely brushing the dust from their linen garments, others still lingered in the cool evening atmosphere contemplating scenes which they are likely to behold but once in a lifetime.

MIRROR LAKE.

THIS beautiful little lake, lying between these gigantic walls, can be reached by a good carriage road, with a short distance to walk. Many persons visit this picturesque piece of scenery without taking the trouble to think why all lakes or ponds are not mirrors. The water, like the Merced, is soft, and clear as crystal, being mostly melted snow. I will here take occasion to say that the wells in the valley seem to be the same quality of water, partaking of the same clearness, coolness and softness. Such water is the greatest luxury upon earth, and its qualities do not cause illness, only from being taken into the system too cold. This lake being encompassed closely by a nich in the walls of the valley, its waters are as placid as the surface of a mirror; not a ripple in seen to disturb its peaceful bosom, unless may be by the jumping of the speckled trout. The time to visit it is between six and seven in the morning. One will never imagine by hearing it spoken of what a perfect looking-glass can be formed of snow water and a dark background. There is no exaggeration in the dimensions of objects, no distortion of shape or color, and no looking-glass could give better satisfaction in portraying images. It must be visited at the right time, for after the sun shines over the walls of the valley it converts this grandest of mirrors into an insignificant fish or frog pond. It has no frogs, however, and the angling tourist and native Indian promise to destroy all the fish, unless some stringent game laws are enacted and rigidly enforced to protect the finny tribes from the above mentioned rapacious monsters. I am told by a resident that the Indians gather the minnows by the half bushel when not more than two or three inches long, and boil them for food. This is certainly a wretched way to destroy these pretty fishes, which should be kept for the benefit of the sporting public, and not for the practical utility of feeding a degraded savage. The depth of this water makes no difference with the perfection of the mirror. The reflection is as perfect where the water is three inches deep as where it is four feet. When the sun can peep over this mighty enclosure, four thousand feet high, it is well to watch the effect of the light upon the trees where it first strikes with concentrated force. Its rays seem to turn the foliage into the most exquisite embossing of silver. This effect is reflected perfectly in the lake, and one can get as fine a view from looking downward as from gazing upward. The rocky walls compose the frame of this wonderful looking-glass. The trees, shrubs and human beings, are as perfectly reflected as from any mirror suspended from the ceiling. There is a kind of rude building, with a platform built out into the edge of the water, and here a small boat is kept, manned by a hopeful young American; and for twenty-five cents one can be rowed out upon this looking-glass, and when the sun is shining its depth is fully revealed, for the pellucid waters can hide nothing.

LEAVING YOSEMITE VALLEY.

AT six in the morning the stage is in readiness. We have our breakfast and get in, driving about two miles, where men are at work upon the road. The Mariposa line at this date is not complete, but will be finished and in good running order by the time this writing reaches the public Saddle and pack horses are brought for us to ride two or three miles. After mounting we are informed that a number of blasts are about to be touched off, and the Chinamen come running back and hide themselves beneath the eaves of those steamboat rocks. We turn our horses backward a few feet, and the blasting commences. The reports — a dozen or more — follow in quick succession, and we are informed that the danger is over. The Chinamen creep from their hiding places and resume work; **and** we ride on, not, however, without a feeling that giant powder or nitro-glycerine might be lying in ambush. The powder used in this operation does not cause the stones to fly, but just bursts them open in the most satisfactory manner, leaving them loose to be removed by the pick and shovel. An intelligent Scotchman in our party was much pleased at being a witness to this blasting process, as he considered it quite a feature in his American travels. The trail for a short distance is so fearfully beset with sharp-edged stones, that I soon forgot the fear of latent fire-works in contemplation of new dangers. It is a wonder that the horses pass through such a path without blood upon their legs; but I heard of no accident.

Here we have upon one hand the refreshing Merced, really swelled to the dignity of a river. The waters are tranquil, and of a lovely green color. Speckled trout were plainly to be seen disporting themselves in the clear water. If those fishes had passed through the foaming cascades which we had visited a day or two before, I do not think there would be many spots left upon them. There is much fording to be done about the Yosemite, the streams being narrow, deep and clear, the banks often very steep, and the waters have quite a current and seem so swashy that one feels as if there were surely a swimming prospect ahead.

There is a little plant, of very thrifty growth, known as the Scotch Cap or thimble berry. This covers the ground in some places; is now in bloom, having a white blossom. The berries will be very plentiful in a few weeks. My late experience has cured me entirely of a desire to go berry hunting. Birds are so scarce in these high altitudes and gummy forests that fruit is secure from their depredations. Wherever there are trees, and fields of grain cultivated, the birds are quite numerous. There are no seedy weeds, and but limited undergrowth in these forests, because of the long dry season. There is not even a great variety of trees, what there are being mostly gum trees, and standing in groups, very free from underbrush; still the shade is thick enough to be complete. Tourists often remark the continued fine weather of this climate;

one's plans are never frustrated because of storms of either wind or rain. If the hotels are crowded, and a room cannot be obtained, it is not thought a hardship to take a blanket and lie down any place where one's person is safe. The children of a family frequently sleep upon the open porch of the house, this being their only bedroom for the entire summer season. I was observing a bed of this description, where the children — three little boys — had just risen to dress. It was a delightfully cool morning, bracing and healthful, and a family of dear little chickens came upon the bed and cuddled down between the blankets and pillows, spreading their wings to catch the animal heat which had not escaped, at the same time cooing and saying all manner of sweet chickadee things. The chickens were up in the morning a long time before the children were, had been to breakfast, and were now ready for a morning nap.

I had almost forgotten that we were really leaving the glorious old Yosemite, a kind of garden of Eden without cultivation; but we must chat a little while slowly winding our way through the shady forest and across deep-seated streams. We have passed the great light-colored rock called the El Capitan — that is if we can pass it while in the valley. Some of these large rocks are like the moon or stars — one may travel half the length of the vale, still they will be ever present. This fact goes far to prove their unappreciated magnitude. The El Capitan is three thousand three hundred feet high; and I will venture to assert that it is the most singular formed mass of matter on the face of the globe. One thing that makes it appear most wonderful is its apparent smoothness and the fact that it differs in color so much from its immediate surroundings, being the shade of fine, thick, light-brown wrapping paper. In the polished sides of this monster, niches are to be seen where good sized trees are growing. Coming in upon the Coulterville route, imagination conjures up a figure upon the surface of this bowlder representing a man with priestly robes and flowing beard. This figure is known as the Wandering Jew. One feels like addressing the El Capitan as an animated creature, although it has not the form of anything in the heavens, upon the earth, or under the earth; still it has a head, face, sides, top and sloping back part. The matter that was once in close proximity must have loosened its hold and slid into the abyss below, which received the retreating earth, leaving these mighty side walls and low valley.

I am inclined to think that if some mining shaft were located near, pieces of El Capitan affinities might be discovered a few hundred feet below. As it is, its individuality is as marked as if there had never been another particle of rock created bearing the least resemblance to this mighty patrician. There are discolored spots upon its sides suggesting the romantic idea that mother nature, in some of her quaking freaks, had upset the ink bottle from a nich or window-sill, and its contents had flowed freely over the delicate shades of El Capitan. Opposite is the Cathedral Rock. This vast pile I admire more than any rock in the valley except the Cap of Liberty. Its well defined spires, its moss covered sides, color and general shape give it the appearance of a ruined cathedral, grand

and beautiful even in desolation. An unsophisticated but pretentious guide imposed upon the honest credulity of a party of tourists by stating that these spires were called the Roman Candles. This rock, although opposite the El Capitan, and perhaps a mile or two apart and a river flowing between, are as different in quality, color and form as if created upon different planets. Trees, grass and trailing vines have sprung up among the Cathedral ruins, and the body of the supposed church is spotted all over with a fine black moss, which gives it the appearance of being ornamented with black velvet buttons. Near this old pile the beautiful Bridal Veil appears. This fall has also a voice, but differing so much from the others that one can hardly recognize it as belonging to the family of waterfalls. It is a clear, distinct, indiscribable sound, more like that made by the running gear of machinery than like the falling of a mighty sheet of water. When it breaks upon the sight it seems like an animated creature calculated to enliven and give variety to its surroundings, those dumb, quiet, magnificent, rocky giants.

While fording one of the many streams in our path, I cast my eyes up to the fall, and, to my delight and surprise, saw it overshadowed with a bright halo, like those represented in the imaginary pictures of Christ and his disciples. The morning sun shining upon the rising mist caused this beautiful phenomenon, and in the after part of the day brilliant rainbows encircle the fall like a skirt of shaded cashmere. This sheet descends nine hundred and forty feet, is one of the highest among the slender variety and appears like rockets coming down head foremost, the wake or tail lingering behind like that of a comet. It has also a sweet, wholesome breath, is a free-will dispenser of the ordinance of baptism, as no one can approach its majestic presence without submitting to this sacred rite. Its misty blessings fall alike upon the just and the unjust, as much as to say, who is competent to judge the wicked.

We now pass on, enjoying the cool, shady nooks, the flowing rivulets, and secluded moss covered rocks, the trees with an occasional sinewy root bared just to give one an idea of their grasping power upon earth. Now we are again upon one of those fearful mountain trails: not precipitous, however, but steep, dusty and filled with rolling stones which gather no moss. The mules are equal to the occasion, going cautiously along, stopping stark still to exchange greetings with others of their kind who have, with much cunning and perversity, hid themselves among the rocks until the hour of mule hunting had passed, and they now had ventured forth to browse and graze in quiet comfort. Josephus, the aged historic mule which I rode, proved himself capable of the passion of jealousy; for, after seeing the others, he bolted out of the trail several times and commenced eating the brush as if he intended to get even as he journeyed.

I reasoned with him; stating, as best I could, that many conditions arise outside of mule society that are unjust and very galling; but that superior creatures often submitted uncomplainingly to those conditions. Notwithstanding all this fine talk I rather respected the mule for showing sufficient sense to bolt and assert himself.

Upon reaching the end of the trail we find an encampment of about a hundred Chinamen at work making the new road. Here I beheld my first blue-tailed lizzard. The colors were so decidedly bright and blue that I could scarcely think of anything else for an hour. Women and girls have been maliciously accused, by the sterner sex, of creating, in Berlin wool, blue-tailed dogs and impossible General Washingtons, but as I never saw one of the aforesaid dogs, am inclined to think it a wicked and slanderous invention of a class ever ready to encourage the most frivolous occupations for my sex, and as ready to jeer and ridicule the worthless results. We are perfectly safe in producing blue-tailed lizzards, however, although I could scarcely have believed my senses. If I had not been credibly informed that they are a distinct speci , and plentiful among the rocks of these mountains, I should have thought this one an accident in nature.

Here we dismount, turn our saddled mules out to graze while waiting for the incoming passengers to take them back upon the trail we have just traversed. After looking about for awhile for a convenient place to take our lunch, one of the Chinamen called out, "John, John," in order to attract the attention of the gentleman, who turned and followed the Celestial, and was shown a tent apparently fitted up for the occasion, as there was a large flat stone for a table, this being surrounded by smaller ones for seats. After thanking the Chinaman, and congratulating ourselves, we spread the board and took our lunch. The Chinaman brought us hot tea in little China bowls, and declined taking pay or money as a gift. After lunch the guide borrowed from the Chinaman a box for me to sit upon, and I had found a shady nook beneath a bank and was chatting with a resident of the mountains and our guide, two middle aged men, possessing much local information. The younger guides were over in the road, scuffling like a litter of half grown cur pups, and swearing apparently for amusement, just as people employ any accomplishment, music for instance, for their own enjoyment, expecting to be heard by others also. After a while we were startled by noisy conversation and the sound of blows, as if the playing had ended, as it usually does, in an angry fight. I sprang up the bank which hid the contestants from view, and saw a Chinaman holding fast to a blanket, while one of the guides was kicking him most unmercifully. The Chinaman came twice to the ground, but made no resistance, only hastened away clinging to the blanket. In spite of my veneration and awe for everything that has a vote and wears breeches, I screamed out, "What are you doing, you rascally guide? Stop kicking that Chinaman!" And he did stop, and if he had not I should have transformed myself into a setting hen and been on his back in another minute. Of course he pretended not to hear anything that had been remarked by outsiders, and began to throw stones at some other Celestials. I sincerely think there is no absurdity or inconsistency that is equal the conceit of the American democrat. When I, with a woman's impulse, started for the field of action, armed with the instincts of justice and humanity, those men that I had been talking with said to me, "Don't go, those fellows may insult you." "Great guns!" I replied, "the vanity of the bewhiskered! Why, sir, a donkey might bray at one, or kick a body, but who would ever think of this act as an insult. What an idea, that any person could be insulted by words coming from the mouth of a profane, illiterate boor, because he belonged to the genus pantaloons. Those ignorant, blaspheming asses; why, they are no more responsible than so many orang-outangs, and when they become physically dangerous should be placed in irons, as they usually are, and led out and hanged like dogs, as many of them are."

While this conversation was going on for the edification of the supercillious American democrat, one of the men took occasion to ask me if I was a "free lover." This was a little unexpected digression from the subject, but when a woman undertakes to reason with a voter, there is no answering for the logical results. Said I, "if I say I am a free lover, of course you will say that you are one also," and before he had time to settle this point, some one came and told us what caused the trouble between the Chinaman and guide. The latter had taken the blanket without permission from the Celestial's tent, and the Chinaman had money rolled up in his blanket and was anxiously looking for it when he desired the guide to get off his blanket; the guide answered that he should not do it, and the Chinaman jerked it from under him, this exasperated the dignity of the insignificant representative of the superior race so much that his injured manhood could not refrain from kicking the poor, skinny old Chinaman.

While I was doubly engaged righting the wrongs of common humanity and assailing the prejudices against my own sex, one of the younger Chinamen commenced to curse the guides. This fellow's attempt to profane the Christian Deity, and consign his enemies to their own eternal blazes, was the most complete farce that I ever witnessed, and I laughed heartily, notwithstanding the prospects were good for a bloody riot. The Chinamen were gathered in groups all over the encampment. Their angry voices could be heard vociferating their threats, and the guides becoming alarmed, had relapsed into deathly silence, nervously waiting the action of the hostile Chinamen, or the arrival of the expected stages loaded with passengers which might have the effect to put a stop to the proceedings. The overseer acknowledged that the Chinamen were getting beyond his control. They had already produced several pistols among them, a fearful looking old horse pistol, about two feet long. Directly the profane Chinaman who tried so hard to imitate the guides, came quietly and respectfully up to me and talked of the row. I said they had better not fight, as that would make great trouble and get some of them in jail. That I was going direct to Merced, would see the General Superintendent, and likely he would discharge the rascally guide who had abused the Chinaman. That good people did not want to have the Chinamen hurt, and would not tolerate the fact of their being ill treated. While I was consoling this Celestial, a score of these little men came and seated themselves upon a burnt log lying near, while I occupied the little cracker box, and talked words of comfort and encouragement. Presently the spokesman of the party asked me to repeat what I had said to him, which I did, and he removed his hat, thanked me with half a dozen short bows, and said that he would go and tell the rest of his countrymen, and soon after their voices assumed a quiet, peaceful tone, and they cast pleasant glances at me all the while I was in the encampment.

I kept my word, and the superintendent went up next day and settled the difficulty to the satisfaction of the Chinamen. For once there was an unpleasantness and no woman at the bottom of it, but one at the top acting successfully as peace commissioner. After waiting full two hours for the stage we were again upon the road. Among the incoming passengers, our Scotch friend discovered a countryman, and although they were not acquainted at home, they greeted one another like brothers.

The initiated related to the stranger about how the trout of the valley were to be captured, stating that the water is so clear and deep that the line must be inked and that the fly must be black, as they do not take to light colored bait and require different management entirely from the

LEAVING YOSEMITE VALLEY. 197

fishes at home. Now we are fairly out upon the Mariposa Road, one of the best mountain thoroughfares in the State. The timber is very fine all along this route, and one can but regret that at present it is inaccessible for commercial purposes. Here, in these forests, I saw my first snow plant, and it appeared the most out of place of anything that I ever observed in nature. This plant is a bulbous, fungus kind of a growth, standing about eight or ten inches high, and in clusters or families like the present trees. Perhaps vegetation combines its strength this way, in order to secure more moisture. The stem of the snow plant is shaped like a variety of cactus called the pyramid cactus, and is as red as blood, and upon this little monument small bell formed flowers appear at regular intervals, but close as they can stand. The whole plant looks like red wax, the petals, stamens, all being of a dark, bright red. This curious vegetable, without a green leaf suggests the idea that it might be a growing monument, springing from the dry, brown soil to honor the memory and blood of heroes and martyrs who may in some worthy cause have moistened the soil with the life current. This plant frequently appears along side of patches of snow, but whether it rises out of the snow, I am unable upon reliable authority to state. There were no patches of snow where I saw it growing, although in a cool altitude. At a certain point upon the road a large flat stone is placed upright like a tombstone. This is said to be eight thousand feet above the level of the sea.

We reach Clark's at six o'clock, a hotel owned by the company and kept on purpose for the accommodation of tourists. Here we tarry for the night. The house is commodious and pleasantly situated. A brisk fire is made every night and morning in a large open fire-place. At this altitude frost appears every month in the year. Trout are furnished for the table in abundance, but cooked in refuse grease in such a manner, that none but the hardiest could retain them upon the stomach. It is a disgrace to the company that this rare and dainty dish, supplied so abundantly in this locality should be served so as to be unpalatable. For many persons the fishes have as great a charm as anything in the valley, and the way they are served leaves nothing for the memory but disappointment and disgust. The next morning we find saddled horses waiting for us to climb another mountain trail, a distance of about six miles, in order to see the Mariposa Big Trees, the grove which the government donated to the State for the benefit of the public.

We have another enjoyable forest ride, where the sugar pine lifts its stately head to the sun and spreads its graceful branches, sporting as if at finger tips, a cluster of the largest and most beautiful cones among the pine family. There is a variety known as the Digger pine which bears a small nut used by the Indians as an article of food. The nut grows between the scales of the pine cone, and is easily rattled out upon a cloth. They are then stored in cribs made of boughs and sticks, something like a big rude corn crib, and kept for use at all seasons of the year. At eleven o'clock we reach a spring of this delightful mountain water, and stop for lunch, supposing that we are at the Big Trees.

Here lies one fallen giant, a victim of fire which burned its roots, loosened its hold upon earth, and caused it to topple over. A wagon could be driven the distance of two hundred feet upon this prostrate trunk. We reach the top of the fallen log by means of a ladder of the length of a common house ladder twelve or fourteen feet. The bark is beaten into a kind of down by the feet of tourists and looks as if it might be invaluable for mouse nests.

This tree is called Andrew Johnson, because it leans toward the South and because its top was shattered in falling. Our guide proves to be a treasure. He is middle aged, a man of good sense and much fine humor, takes excellent care of his horses, and helps to entertain parties with a fund of jocular stories or sound information if required. While we were taking our lunch he told how the bluejays and woodpeckers make their sandwiches. They first peck the bark of a tree full of holes, then proceed to fill these perforations with acorns; these are then left until the worms begin to work in them, when the birds consider them fit for use, as this provides them with both bread and meat at once in the form of a sandwich. He also related what he declared was a fact about the birds filling nuts into a hollow tree; that he discovered them at work like so many bees, flying back and forth; that he bored a hole in the tree where it would strike the hollow, and fastened a sack at the opening; that the nuts kept rolling into this sack, and that he used them to feed his fattening swine. When pressed to tell how and when the birds discovered this fraudulent operation, he refused to state, saying that there was no use of his trying to be entertaining, because we were so skeptical. I imagined the lonesome cry of these disgusted bluejays when they discovered that the bottom had fallen out of the bin holding their treasures, and the shrill shriek of the sorrowing woodpecker as he lifted his fiery smoking cap above the tops of these lofty pines, and went sailing round chirping a disconsolate wail, evidently so demoralized as to be unable to determine which way to fly or what to do next. Poor birds! poor birds! Man's inhumanity to birds, etc.

As I was worrying my brain trying to find

something to rhyme with Burns without quoting his direct words, I cast my eyes upward, and discovered an opening in a tree about twenty feet from the ground, and this place was filled with uncorked bottles, clinched in so firmly that if our guide had told us that they were placed there by the avenging bluejay, and driven home by the angry woodpecker, I should have been half inclined to believe the story. The guide did relate to us the circumstance which brought the bottles there to our satisfaction. When a party had partaken of champagne until they became merry, they made bets as to who could make a bottle stick, and what we saw was the results. From the shallow nature of the cleft in the tree one would think it almost impossible to make a bottle stay; hence it appeared something of a feat, and in all probability several efforts were made upon each subject before it could be induced to take a sticking position. There is a small log house erected at this point, making a sleeping place for hunters, as grizzly bears and California lions are still too numerous in these mountain retreats to think of trusting one's person to sleep without protection.

The big trees in this location are mostly named, many of them after the different Western States. Indiana, Ohio, Iowa, Illinois, and several other States were represented. Any person is permitted to name the trees, as it makes the groves more interesting. Parties desiring the names to become permanent must send a sign with the cognomen painted on it, and it will be placed upon the tree. Some persons have sent beautiful white marble, handsome enough for a door plate. Some of the names are upon plated metal, but most are upon jappaned tin, and placed high enough upon the tree to prevent malicious depredations.

After our lunch and story telling is ended we are told to mount our horses again, that we are going now through the real grove of big trees. For my part I thought with P. T. Barnum, that if they had anything larger than Andy Johnson to show that we had better take chloroform. These trees are not so tall in proportion as the pine, nor are they as deep rooted; and if a fire gets about the roots their hold upon earth for an upright position is slight, but they must ever remain a wonder for the world. There are seven or eight hundred in this grove, and this number being so near together is no less a wonder than their size. They are just the color of the earth, and one would think the soil upon which they stand exhausted forever from producing these monstrosities. It is a subject of much regret that these trees have been so injured by fire; but when one thinks of the matter, it is the greatest wonder of all how they could possibly escape being burned to the ground, and that the whole forest has not perished in the same way because of the long dry season, these trees being of the most inflammable kinds of timber, and the bark as light and dry as punk. The reason that these forests have not succumbed to fire is because there is very little underwood, and no rank grasses or growth of vegetation to feed the devouring element in its infancy or while it is creeping; and fire does not climb trees well until it is strong as a giant, backed closely by allies and immediate reinforcements. We spend a couple of hours in looking at the trees, riding among them. I will say little about the size of them, for there are regular scientific works to be had giving accurate information; but one of these trees, reader, is as large as five or six of the largest trees you ever saw put together. I fancied that our whole party looked wall-eyed for several days after visiting the big trees. It certainly expands one's ideas of things, and makes one almost ready to believe anything.

We play circus by riding our horses through a fallen tree trunk about fifty feet long. This tree had been burned out, forming a cylinder while lying down. Our guide shows me a very fine perfect tree, not more than half as large as some other — perhaps twelve feet in diameter — and said that I might christen this with some name. I called it Minnesota, after the North Star State. Soon we come to another giant or handsome perfect tree, and the guide called to the Scotch gentleman, saying that he might bestow some name upon this. The Scotchman lifted his hat and bowed, answering, "No such desecration." "O, fie," said I, "upon your Scotch perversity; name the tree, call it Robert Burns." "Well," said he, "you name it." This, I think, was said that the diffident gentlemen might not be called upon for anything like ceremony in the presence of the company — such a majestic platoon, mounted upon dignified, fierce-looking steeds. The animals had all halted, waiting the action of the guide, who had turned about to settle this matter. I then took advantage of the audience, and called in a voice as if addressing a thousand persons, "Ladies and gentlemen, that this tree shall henceforth and forever be known as Robert Burns, the peasant poet of Scotland, in respect to the Scotch gentleman now visiting us; any person having objections, let them be stated now, or forever hereafter hold their peace." The company raised their hats, gave three cheers for Robert Burns, and went their way. The horses now begin to realize that they are headed homeward, and quicken their steps until they become brisk walkers.

At six P. M. we are again at Clark's, where we remain over night, and at half-past five are upon the road for Merced. The obliging driver gave me the choice of a seat upon the outside, and came near having a scene with a San Francisco ruffian in order to keep his promise. Gallantry prevailed, however, even toward the strong-minded, and I take the seat of war and retain it, while the ruffian is compelled to find a place in another vehicle belonging to the same company.

Upon this route of sixty-eight miles we change horses six or seven times and reach Merced at five o'clock. The coaches are new and handsome, the horses are selected and matched with much care and taste, five being driven at once, three leaders and two wheelers. In one of the changes a Canadian pony was brought out and placed alongside of the other leaders. I immediately recognized a native of my own country and watched the movements of this compact built piece of horse flesh with much interest. The driver says that this little creature has out-worked three common teams already, and is still good for a summer's labor. It had such a baby or colty look beside the other horses, that I just wish it were possible for me to purchase the creature and place it in some horse heaven, abounding in clear streams and alfalfa grass, where it should do no more staging. When stopping to change, the greatest possible speed was used in getting the horses out of harness and the fresh ones in, as the driver was determined not to allow the stage containing the San Francisco chap to pass. A passenger became interested, dismounting from his seat upon top of the coach and assisting about the harness every time a change was made. The driver, a good fellow in the main, showed some symptoms of emotional insanity upon this occasion, as he would let nothing pass him nor permit other teams to remain long ahead. One poor old codger who was somewhat inspired came near getting a thrashing for running his horses in order to keep ahead until he reached his own home. The driver showed us a ravine where his team saw a grizzly bear last summer. The monster was taking his breakfast from the carcass of a dead mule which was lying in the ravine. The horses saw him and became frantic; they started upon a run, the driver found it impossible to hold them, although he could keep them upon the road, they ran all the way to the next station and were trembling with fear and excitement when taken from the harness, casting suspicious glances about, as if they momently expected to be eaten alive. There was but one passenger in the coach and the driver said that he occupied all the seats in the vehicle, and sometimes all of them at once. There was no time for an explation, and the passenger did not find out the cause of the unusual haste until they arrived at the station. That team refused afterwards to pass this ravine where the grizzly breakfasted, and were changed and put upon another route. I am half inclined to think that those horses had been demoralized listening to bugaboo stories told by superstitious drivers for the entertainment of over credulous travelers. The mountains here are used as one vast range for sheep and goats. Skirmishes occasionally arise between herders as to whom shall retain certain localities. As we change altitudes the mountain formation, soil and vegetation changes. We pass through the Fremont estate, the famous Mariposa grant. There was once a fine flourishing town here, but like most of its mining cotemporaries, has fallen into decay and ruin. A fifty stamp quartz mill, one of the best modern structures in this State, stands the reverses of time like the dignified head of a great house, only the more susceptible parts showing decline, such as the window glass and discoloring of the paint. The little churches remind me of the fine weather-worn physiognomies of some of the old bachelors of this country, known as the knights of forty-nine, and it will be the regret of my life that I did not tarry a week at Mariposa. The climate is in the altitude to be most delightful, and the bachelors ever ready to sacrifice themselves in order to impart information to lady writers. Many of these heroes still live, many of them wealthy and gallant, with good health and fine eyes; men who have braved the temptations of frontier life and come safe and sound through the lonely clouds of unsocial life and years of social privations. I have met many such and sometimes regret that I am not a marrying subject. Believing as I do in the Darwinian theory, and knowing as I do that I have not thrown off the sitting hen stage of evolution, I will accept no offer of marriage until hen pecking becomes more popular. We stop but ten minutes at this delightful, at the same time dilapidated, town. At two o'clock we dine at a little place called Hornitos, a Spanish settlement. The hotel is kept by a Scotchman whose name is McDougal. Having a real woman for a wife this house is well kept, one of the best in the State. There is little in this world successfully accomplished without the refining influence and personal assistance of woman, and this house is a worthy example; the food is first class, and one does not think the charges high for such accommodations, and in this location. Nearing the plains, the whole nature of the landscape becomes changed; the water is poor, and already we begin to thirst for the beautiful Merced and its pebbly tributaries. The plains here for several miles are the most fearfully barren country under the sun; nothing more so unless it be a sandy desert. To be sure the grass springs up once a year green and fresh; it is short lived, however, leaving a dead brown all over the earth, relieved by a rocky formation of a most dismal aspect, appearing like an old cemetery with its head and footstones leaning every way, evincing the neglect that comes to the dead with years. The only living thing seen upon this desolate waste is the small brown birds which live like highway robbers, by what they can pick up on the road. Notwithstanding all this barrenness, the locality is mostly productive, and with irrigation, can be made to produce like a garden, and much of this very kind of desolation has been improved within the last five years. Trees can be grown so rapidly that little is thought of settling up some of these barrens where water can be procured. We reach Merced at five, having beaten the other stage one hour, and driven sixty-eight miles in ten hours. The party look like wilted poppies, or a dust-covered, faded bouquet, and pass off sullenly to their rooms, without exchanging a word, only wondering that any one could endure all this fatigue and find themselves alive in the morning.

THE VISALIA BRANCH OF THE CENTRAL PACIFIC RAILROAD.

LATHROP is the name of the station where this branch connects with the Central Pacific Railroad. The towns Modesto, Merced, Fresno, Visalia and Bakersfield are all upon this line of road. Much of the country presents a dreary, barren appearance; but a chain of mountains are in sight, containing a supply of water that is to be the means of settling up these vast plains. For miles the surface is as level as a house floor, appearing like packed sand. A true statement in regard to this smoothness seems almost incredible. It could not have been reduced to a more perfect level with a field roller. Adjoining this plain little mounds appear, at first very low, increasing in size until they remind one of the prairie dog villages or musk-rat tenements; this formation continues for miles. At first I thought some farmer had dumped compost in heaps upon the ground, leaving it to decompose for the purpose of enriching the soil, but as the train whirls past thousands of acres of these little hillocks I begin to think that it is another of California's monstrosities. Gradually these mounds become less, disappearing for the wonderful smooth level. These singular features must have been formed by the action of water upon a loose, movable soil. In spite of the dreary, barren appearance of the great plains they are becoming settled much faster than one would suppose if not acquainted with their real resources. Little groves of shades are appearing along, nearest the foot-hills, gradually pushing out upon the open plains. dwellings .nestle in these shades, making an oasis of fertility upon the hitherto bleak desert. Shade and fruit trees can be grown so rapidly that the supply of water and a title to the land are the most important things to be considered; for legislative acts take away the necessity of fencing, and the soil can be tilled by machinery almost entirely. The steam plow may be driven to great advantage, and there are neither sticks nor stones to interfere with reaper and mower; and the fertility of this apparently barren soil is not to be questioned, as it has been thoroughly tested.

These plains were formerly used entirely for grazing purposes. Herdsmen came with large droves of cattle that fed upon the tender grass that came forth during the winter rains. At present legislation has been in favor of protecting the agricultural interests, and the cattle, like the Indians, must be driven further away into inaccessible wilds or where the rugged formation makes the prospect for cultivation quite hopeless.

Modesto is a trading point for Stanislaus county as well as the county seat. Merced is also a county seat, and is rejoicing in a new and very handsome court house. This is one of the principal points from which the famous Yosemite is reached. It is surrounded for miles by wheat fields, and shades are extensively planted.

Fresno is another county seat, belonging to Fresno county. This is a flourishing shanty town just in that stage of semi-civilization when feminine virtue is a thing fearful to contemplate. A lady book agent relates a good story of this place, and as it contains a moral I will reproduce it for the benefit of other rural localities. The lady put up at the hotel and remained for several days; none of the women about the house ventured to speak to her, and only cast sidelong glances "of a dredful suz" nature. One afternoon a party of a dozen or more of these matrons and maids had convened for some kind of a buzzing bee. Few of them had been favored with a sight so rare and strange as a woman traveling without the protection of corduroy, and some of them desired to get a peep at the creature. The woman of the house, poor thing, by the way, is a married woman and had set her face against single women who travel alone and put up at hotels, fearing that in spite of her charms that another woman could, if so disposed, take advantage of the infirmaties of her John; so of course, her energies were exerted to protect John, which was all right and proper; just as it should be. The protection is much more frequently upon this hand then upon the other, notwithstanding the assumption of all Johns to the contrary. Well, to the story: The dame informed her guests that there was an aperture in the door of the lady's room, one that she had caused to be made for reasons best known to herself; that the company could repair to the second floor and file along the hall to the front porch, every one taking a peep as she passed. Each one placed her hands under her bustle, as if to keep them unspotted from all wickedness on venturing one eye upon a thing of so doubtful a nature. Unfortunately, but quite naturally the scene proved too ridiculous for the gravity of some of the younger ones, who giggled outright when the first brave was peeping. The lady, upon hearing the noise in the hall, open her door very unexpectedly before the first of the file had time to resume a normal attitude. The girls snickered, the matrons were struck dumb with suppressed virtue, while they leaned their backs against the wall and gazed until the lady had made a run down a flight of stairs, given some order and returned. Such virtue and awe are perfectly awful.

I had, myself, some serious difficulty in conforming to the local customs of this particular place. The train reached this point at midnight and a public vehicle conveys passengers to a hotel. Besides myself, there was another individual possessed of sufficient audacity to be a female and to arrive at this town at that unseemly hour of the night. This woman was a southwesterner, of the lean, lank kind; one whose forefathers had been reared among the North Carolina pines, and had caught the inspiration for a lofty carriage. She was so destitute of adipose tissue that I thought she was in the last stages of consumption. Thin as a shadow, with glassy black eyes, she was anything but a pleasing spectacle to encounter at this stilly hour of night. In due time we were seated in the parlor, waiting to be shown to our rooms. The skeleton woman had asked several characteristic questions; such as, were my parents alive and well, whether I did not want to see them, etc.

I was tired, sleepy, and not particularly amiable, and feeling the iron grasp of social intolerance, I rushed out of the room into the bar, supposed to be headquarters, in order to find some one to show us rooms. The first thing that burst upon my sleepy vision was a row of men standing at the counter with glasses raised ready to take a drink. Said I to the man behind the bar, "Why don't you show us women our rooms? What is your object in keeping us sitting up the rest of the night?" The proprietor answered in an apologetic tone, "We only came in here to register our names, ma'am." "Well," said I, "it takes a very long time for you to register, considering that you are supposed to only be able to make your mark." Said he, "It took some time to mix the fluids." Said I, "Yes, and it will take more time to wipe those glasses." The fellow trembled, but managed to wipe the glasses, casting fearful glances at me in the meantime. At last he looked for a room and returned, saying that there was but one vacant, and asked me if I would have any objection to sharing my bed with the strange woman. "Great guns!" I exclaimed, "I would as soon lie down in the embrace of death. If you had not rooms for us, why did you bring us here and never notify us until everybody is in bed at the other public houses?" I made use of some of the most decided expressions that I had ever added to my vocabulary. The result was that I was shown the room without more words. I felt a little uneasy for the comfort of the other woman, fearing that she might die before morning, but that uneasiness did not amount to enough to turn my room into a public hospital. I afterwards learned that she was hung upon a hook in the hall to keep the breeze from wafting her away in the dark; at daylight she was taken down and placed in a reclining position upon a sofa with her extremities upon the floor; in this attitude she was found when the servants opened the parlor door in the morning. I was told afterward that this woman was not an invalid; that this thinness was normal; that she had the nervous vital temperament, and could adapt herself to almost any condition or circumstance. While I tarried here the hotel proprietor would dodge involuntarily every time he saw me coming, always finding business in another direction. I occasionally meet a wedding party at hotels where I am stopping, and can always tell them from other people because the waiter in the dining-room tips up the chairs at their table, and because the bride hangs on the bridegroom's arm in a languishing manner. This looks very silly, and my opinion is that the beauty of being newly married is to behave as if it were nothing unusual; appear as much like old married folks as possible, not speaking or taking any notice of one another only when it is impossible to avoid it. I have just another word to say in regard to young people marrying -- that is, that lady teachers shall not marry men who are teachers also, it is not a profitable cross. Supposing the children should inherit a double dose of pedantry and be obliged from early life to wear glasses and walk stiff-legged, what would they be good for? At Tulare I was apprised of a singular circumstance that may be of public interest; that there is a swine-herder in that vicinity by the name of Ham, black by name and nature, truly a queer coincidence. Visalia, the county seat of Tulare county, lies about a mile from the railroad. It has three thousand inhabitants, mostly southerners and southwesterns. There is a great number of old men in this place; likely those who have been impoverished by the calamities of war and found homes here in this warm climate where less exertion is required to procure a livlihood, and the warm climate is conducive to longevity. Visalia and the country around has the most beautiful and extensive groves of the native oak that I have observed in the whole State of California. The inhabitants have had the bad taste to cut down many of these elegant trees and plant little stripling fancy shades in their places. These noble trees were made on purpose to shade the earth and form an asylum for man and other animals, and no ornamental tree can ever serve this purpose as well. Wheat is grown extensively in this region. The grapes are too sweet for wine making, are only fit for raisins. The weather gets very hot during summer, being away from ocean breezes and the altitude is not sufficient to modify a tropical sun as it does in some localities. While staying in this place I had a cat adventure which I will relate, as it may throw some light upon the habits of domestic animals in this region. My window opened upon the roof of another part of the building; at midnight I heard a sound as if some person were trying to get in. Springing from my bed in terror, I exclaimed, "Who is there?" at the same time passing my head out of the casement. I saw nothing but a large yellow cat, and it answered in the most placid manner with a long rolling purr. I said to him, "What are you doing around here at this time of night." The cat answered meekly, as well as cats can, that he was looking for another feline which had been lost for several days. I accepted this as an excuse, thinking it better than none, but closed my window, not however without saying a few words of comfort to the lonely wanderer that duty called into this midnight service.

MONTEREY.

THIS quaint old town was the former county seat of Monterey county. It is handsomely situated upon the southern part of the bay of the same name; has nearly or quite four thousand inhabitants, and is one of the most wonderfully contrived collections of houses to be seen this side of Mexico. If the buildings had been dropped down from the moon, one house at a time, it could not present a more deranged conglomeration. They are mostly of the old Spanish style, the material adobe, the shape long, low and porched, and plastered upon the outside; white in color, with tiled roofs, and little prism like windows set in the thick walls with iron bars running up and down like those on our insane asylums. The rafters for the roofs are tied in place by thongs of untanned bullock's hide, which have stood the storms of a century, and may be good for another. The tiled roofs are a great curiosity to persons not accustomed to seeing them. The tiles are of a light brick or cinnamon color, and look like long earthen flower pots, split in two lengthwise, or like a length of red earthen stove pipe (if one can imagine such a thing), and then split it lengthwise. The lower row placed with concave side upwards, the upper row with concave side downwards, forming little troughs for carrying off the water. The bark of trees have been used in the same manner for primitive dwellings and out buildings. In fact these tiles suggest the idea of huge rolls of cinnamon bark placed upon the roof to cure.

Some of these Monterey structures stretch half the length of a block or more, with no way of reaching the back yard, unless entrance is made at the front door, or one must pass clear around "Robin Hood's barn." The doors and windows occur at regular intervals, and the fronts have the strictly secluded appearance of a nunnery. I am not certain whether one of these blocks are owned by a single proprietor, or if the ancient builder joined walls with his neighbor; if the latter supposition be true, the joining was very smoothly done.

Observing a card upon one of the numerous doors, announcing "To let, or for sale," I wondered if this referred to one compartment or the whole long row. There is no regularity in the streets. In some places the thoroughfare must continue alongside of a house very straight, then its course is interrupted by a three cornered structure standing just where the road should continue ; the consequence is, there is a branching off each side of the impediment, and an angle taken in some unexpected direction. A few buildings stand protruding cornerwise into the street. One comes to the conclusion that every man caused his lot to face which way it best pleased him, and that no two fronts consecutively in one direction. A few of the gardens are enclosed with a wall of stone five or six feet in height. These have the appearance of jail yards, and completely obscure from sight the growth of vegetation in them. These enclosures include the back part of the house, and have one other entrance, a ponderous old fashioned gate, which is falling into decay, having a slothful, neglected appearance. Most of them have outlived their curious hinges and are propped up by a rail or in some unwarlike manner, for everything about the place proves the necessity of fortifications in an early day against Indians, wild beasts and the thieving laymen of the established church. The population of Monterey is as mixed and irregular as are its buildings and thoroughfares; being composed of Spaniards, Italians, Old Californians, Digger Indians, French, German, Irish, English and Americans. The Catholic is the prevailing faith, hence newspapers have a fitful existence and generally die young. This place was the early home of Vasques, the notorious robber. For a general thing the Spaniards seem to have no visible means of support. If a circus comes that way their last chicken will be sold to defray the expenses of the entertainment. To justify themselves in becoming marauders, many of them speak of the American with a sense of injury, after the manner of the "noble red man," as if he were an unwelcome intruder who had defrauded them of their birth-right and swindled them out of the chance of competition in the race of life. The idiosyncracies of this people are as peculiar as their structures and streets.

I could scarcely leave my hotel and turn a corner without being lost, in the tortuous meanderings of the deviating ways of its thoroughfares. A young goose strayed from the flock within the sound of their answering voices screamed and called for half a day, evidently in great trouble, running back and forth and returning every few minutes to the spot from whence she started. At last I concluded that it was hardly just to expect a goose to know more of these streets than the people do, although hatched and bred within its crooked and uncertain precincts, so I started off and spent half an hour in getting her back to her sympathizing kindred. When the clan saw us coming they presented a file of snowy breasts and made very low bows, telling in goose latin as best they could, how pleased they were that the prodigal goose had returned. Every one expressed thanks to me

and congratulations to her. I replied in English
that it was no trouble at all, that I was tired of
hearing her lonesome call and the sorrowful echo,
and when I walked away, fancied that one old
gander tried to quote what he remembered of
"Little Breeches," but his mouth was so full of
the tender blades of grass, that I could not distinctly understand.

Monterey will now be somewhat aroused from
its conservative lethargy, as it is the terminus of
a railroad connecting it with San Francisco and
many of the intervening towns upon the coast.
This port was formerly quite a resort for whales,
which came in from the ocean for the chance of
procuring food in the more shallow waters of the
bay. It is said that with this creature the period
of gestation commences in the North, and is
finished in the Southern seas, where the young
ones can be received with a warm bath; that this
is one of their stopping places upon their transit
from ocean to ocean; that they do not call as
frequently as they did twenty years ago, because
they have been mercilessly slaughtered here.
However, I never hear of Monterey but that they

have taken another whale, which the whole population turn out to see, as if it were a novelty. Perhaps the difference in the size of these creatures makes it a novelty to the most experienced. The beach is strewn with the bleaching bones of these sea monsters, and sections of vertebra a foot across are converted into sidewalks, stretching half a block, or the length of an adobe house. It is supposed that only inexperienced, restless young whales, which refuse to follow the advice of their seniors, now put in at this landing, where so many have lost their lives. The town of Monterey is backed by a fine tract of farming land, known as Salinus Valley. Vast quantities of wheat are raised here. The new railroad is just completed, and upon the above date a large vessel had arrived, to be loaded with wheat for the Liverpool market. The arrival was hailed as quite an event, as no vessel of this importance had been seen in this port within the recollection of the middle aged of the present generation. The wharves were not in passable condition, but men were set to work at once to improve them, and new ones are in course of construction. An old rusty cannon was brought out, and a few salutes fired in honor of the event. In the course of six hours the entire population had visited the incomplete wharf to behold the beautiful stranger, which was anchored at such a provoking distance that one could not decipher the name; and as there were so many rash statements made in regard to the number of tons the vessel would carry, I did not dare trust to heresay for the name of the respected visitor.

The great variety of mosses and shells found in this bay are among the curiosities of pleasure seekers who come to this coast, and also of those who are residents of the State. Many come here during summer and camp out, that they may better enjoy the delightful wonders of the sea. The varigated abalone shell is found here and worked into very pretty jewelry by the Spaniards, and sold surprisingly low, considering the fact that they are manufactured by hand — a very tedious process. I was informed by a Yankee jeweler that they could be made with the help of a lathe, which will greatly facilitate the process, and give the poor conservative native another cause for condemning American innovation and enterprise.

OCTOBER.

VALLEJO.

VALLEJO is the principle town in Solano county, is situated on the east side of San Pablo Bay. From San Francisco it is reached by boats running up the bay of the same name. A railroad connects it with the towns of the more northern counties. Vallejo received its name from a Spanish governor of that cognomen, who used to own most of the land about the place. The town is located among the barren hills of the coast range. No verdure greets the eye but that planted by the hands of man. The scenery is mountainous, being the ever occurring round mounds as far as the vision reaches upon one hand, upon the other the placid waters of San Pablo Bay. The town has about six thousand inhabitants, and many characteristic peculiarities; likewise a history of its own.

One of the institutions is known as the Good Templars' Orphans' Home, a fine building, located upon one of those barren hills where the winds sweep with such force as to preclude the possibility of raising shrubbery; for the same reason the children are seldom seen playing in the yards. The building appears to the observer like a grand castle set upon a rock, defying the winds which are said to be tempered to the shorn lamb, although shearing the hills of ever attempt at vegetable growth. This home is supported by the good templars of the State, is managed by women and controlled by a committee of men. There are, at present, about one hundred children in the institution, and notwithstanding the name they are mostly the children of the inebriate. As the temperate man is more capable of providing for his own than the intemperate, there is little necessity of an institution of this kind for the former.

Another of the peculiarities of Vallejo is the navy yard, which is located upon a little oblong island rising from the waters of the bay. This body of land is known as Mare Island, and upon it are situated the navy hospital, the dry dock, the government machine shops and the residences of the naval officers. The grounds are laid out in fine walks with beautiful flowers, many of which bloom the year round. Those naval officers appear to be as well fed dominant set of toadies as ever served a government with good pay for little work. Just before election fifteen hundred or two thousand men are put upon the government works, only to be discharged after their votes are secured. The degrading effects of buying and selling voters is very apparent among the population. or certain features arise from the fact that only the most degraded of men can be bought and sold like so many cattle.

The hospital is without a matron, and when the principal physician was questioned in regard to the selfishness of man for monopolizing all the offices, he replied that women had not yet sufficient political influence to secure a position and hold it. I replied that woman had sufficient political influence to be tried and hung for treason, if not sufficient to receive the emoluments of office. There is many a poor deserving widow of intelligence and refinement that would gladly exchange the drudgery of the needle for such a position, and it rightly belongs to some woman. Our sex should be represented in every department of the government.

Ships are built and repaired upon this island, the timber being brought from Puget Sound. A ferry boat, running every half hour, connects Mare Island with Vallejo proper. The workmen who are employed by the government mostly live in Vallejo, and it is a rare sight to see them trudging past regularly, at eight in the morning and five in the evening, each armed with the inevitable dinner pail. The street is cleared of other pedestrians, there being an expressed aversion to going out at those hours; perhaps because it is never pleasant to meet an army face to face, under any circumstances.

Vallejo was talked of as the capital of the State at one time. There were two sessions of the legislature commenced here, both adjourned to other places to finish — one to Benicia, the home of the famous Benicia Boy, the pugilist, the other adjourned to Sacramento. In moving, the members were obliged to brave both mud and flood, which they did in order to secure the better facilities of the other towns in the way of business excitement, the variety of their fluids and for many unknown reasons. It was not expected by an over generous people that Vallejo could hold, for one entire session, that excitable body of highly intelligent men who are supposed to possess an order of brain that soars far beyond all earthly restraint. The legislature of those days was really a "Circumlocution Office," with the opportunity of putting in practice "How not to do it." Like boys in an ungraded country school, they were permitted to move their seats to any part of the State, in order to avoid what might occur to mar their happiness, from the primitive condition of things. And without doubt, like the school boy, many of the inconveniences became imaginary, and that seats were moved just for the novelty of changing places. The school boy manner still clings to some of the principal men of Vallejo. A citizen and voter, who has yellow curls and golden beard, who looks like a gentleman, upon the outside, and who passes among six foot men for a gentleman, was known to abuse an inoffensive business woman, just as a great, rough, uncouth school boy will sometimes use offensive language to the most sensitive little girl in the class, for the purpose of showing how beauty and the beast appear when chance places them upon the same foraging ground. Vallejo has a parrot, too, which partakes, to some extent, of the peculiarities of the place and the school boy style. I was seated in the office of that estimable gentleman, Colonel Hubbs, and Polly was in her cage, just back of my chair. Presently the bird muttered out: "Polly wants her coat." I asked for an explanation, and was told that she was calling for an old coat that had been placed over her cage to keep her warm. A farmer came in, during the conversation; his hair was rather long, his pants were of a color that would justify me in calling him a Missourian. Polly turned up her eye, took a good look at him, and called out: "How d'ye do, Daddy; how d'ye do, Old Hoss?" At this novel salutation the farmer laughed until the tears came in his eyes.

PLACERVILLE.

THIS fine, handsome, at the same time dilapidated town, is the county seat of Eldorado county, is situated twelve miles north of the Sacramento Valley Railroad, and reached by stages from Diamond Springs, the present terminus of the road. Placerville is a mining town, and twelve or fifteen years ago contained eight or ten thousand inhabitants. As the mining interests changed throughout the State, becoming systematized and consolidated, this place, like all the mountain towns, fell into a rapid decline. Its population will not now number over three thousand. Having the finest climate in the world, like ancient Rome much of its original attractiveness still lingers about the quiet streets, dainty little homes and deserted business buildings. The location and altitude combine to make the atmosphere so sweet that I fancied it had a taste like Bartlett Spring Water. This climate is wonderfully exhilarating. I found myself enduring a walk of many miles with little fatigue, and was surprised that one night's sleep could dissipate the effects of so much exertion.

The inhabitants have fair, clear complexions, and I fancy that they are morally superior to the inhabitants in the valleys. The hoodlum element certainly does not flourish to any great extent, for the window panes of those vacant houses remain unmolested, which fact speaks volumes for the youth of the town.

The inhabitants complain of suffering much from the tyranny of a railroad company; having contributed heavily toward the construction of a road which fails to come to their contract and expectations by a distance of twelve miles. The town is much in debt. In order to escape the penalty of indebtedness, their corporation is dissolved; the town officials resigned as soon as elected. It seems sad to leave those beautiful shades for the pecuniary prospects of the less healthful but more hopeful valleys. If Oliver Goldsmith could have had such a field for his fertile imagination as the ruined or decayed mountain towns of the Golden State, he might have indulged in deserted villages to his heart's content.

Abundance of fruit is raised in the vicinity of Placerville. As the mountain fruits are much superior to that raised in the valley, this commodity generally finds a ready market; is canned, dried, preserved, made into jellies and sold fresh in many parts of the State. Plums are a marvel of variety, size and flavor. I was one day sitting beneath a tree which I supposed to be an apple tree, loaded with green fruit. I reached up to a limb, plucked one, when to my surprise I found a soft green plum as large as a teacup, and of a most excellent flavor, having just the general appearance of a thrifty half grown apple. Blackberries, the fruit of the bramble, are grown in abundance. Indeed, if any care or pains are taken, the finest fruits in the world can be grown here. There is just enough frost to give the apples and peaches a fine flavor which they do not get in the valleys. I was much amused, while stopping there, at a flock of geese, which go about the streets like privileged characters. Every day, in my wanderings, I managed to hold a conversation with these loquacious bipeds. The Beecher scandal was the topic of the day, and to the snowy breasts of these inoffensive birds did I commit my opinions; and the answers which were returned proved quite as satisfactory to me as the general comments of the press, for and against. When I interrogated the geese about the propriety of having every editor in the country arrested for sending obscene literature through the United States mail, the geese all joined together and fairly screamed their approval, crossing their white necks and following alongside of the wooden walks for the distance of a whole block. These and similarly constituted bipeds are the only creatures with whom I enjoy small talk; they are not offensively opinionated upon subjects of which they know comparitively nothing. They seldom or never go beyond their depth while conversing, although fond of water they seldom slop over. These creatures become so readily educated, in a short time, as to give you just the answers required; and to a person intolerent of the opinions of others this fact is highly satisfactory.

SALT LAKE CITY

THE Mormon city contains fifteen or twenty thousand inhabitants. In the entire territory there are about one hundred and fifty thousand persons, one-fifth of this population being Gentiles. A German Jew says, "this is a country where the Jews are all Gentiles." Owing to the peculiar character of the social institutions of this people, the business portion of the city is much smaller than other cities of its population, hence it is a town of extended suburbs. This is perhaps partly owing to the fact that their civilization is in an exceedingly primitive state, and their manner of living decidedly simple, and partly from the fact that their business is conducted upon the co-operative plan, consequently very much concentrated. Salt Lake City is well laid out, with wide streets, beautifully shaded, and a range of mountains forming a picturesque back ground; one of its most charming features being the sparkling rivulets running along each side of its main thoroughfares. The moisture from these brooks is sufficient to cover the banks with a green grassy growth, and the voice of the rippling waters give a peculiar charm to its vicinity. These rivulets are frequently turned aside in their course and used for irrigating gardens, for domestic purposes, and for watering the dusty streets.

My room was near the Museum, in the cottage occupied by Brigham Young's seventeeth wife, Harriet Barney Young. This location is adjacent to the Tabernacle. From my room door I had an excellent opportunity to speculate upon the style of the Tabernacle architecture. It is said that the more elegant architectural structures of a people are always modeled from its first primitive dwellings. For instance, the Chinese Temples were patterns of the round cloth tent; the Gothic houses from the tent of boughs. I cannot, however, imagine anything from which this Mormon Tabernacle could have been modeled, unless it should be a large, oblong, bag pudding, placed upon a platter ready to be served to a goodly number of hungry harvest hands. A people whose highest ideas of life have lain in a plum pudding, may have fashioned their Temple after the same.

The roof is made of shingles and not covered with tin. The block of ground upon which the Tabernacle is placed, is enclosed with a high wall, said to have been first built as a defense against Indians. The Indians were, however, easily reconciled to Mormonism, being already polygamists, and believing in the slavery of women; all they had to do was to be baptized, and they were better Mormons than can ever be made of the Anglo Saxon race; as all orders of the priest-hood have ever found the latter race prone to backslide as soon as they had an opportunity to learn to read. One is surprised to see the great numbers of deformed people upon the streets of Salt Lake City. All manner of deformity is represented here. I thought at first that some institution of malformations were having a holiday, but learned that this feature is the result of the Mormon doctrine of curing by miracles; but for the lack of faith, most of them are bound to go through life warped physically as they have been mentally. The climate of Utah like that of California, is without rain during the summer months, although owing to its altitude it is much colder in winter. The sand storms peculiar to this region is perhaps one of its most objectionable features, although no worse, may be, than the faults of any country. The sweeping wind which Mark Twain denominates the Mountain Zephyr, comes tearing through the valley, filling the air with dust and sand, so that respiration becomes difficult and the inhabitants speedily seek the nearest shelter. These storms have a peculiar hissing sound combined with the roar of the wind and are in miniature what takes place in the great desert of Sahara. Whirlwinds occasionally form, carrying the sand and dust a hundred feet or more into the air. At times three or four of these whirlwinds may be seen waltzing upon the plains at once. As long as they keep a respectful distance, thekcapers are rather edifying, but outsiders never care to have waltzers come too near the corn field. Salt Lake, the dead sea of America, is well worth visiting. It is located about twenty-five miles from the city, is forty miles in length and twenty-five in width, is connected to the city by rail and is famous as a place of resort for the native population. The waters are supposed to possess wonderful curative powers, which would be nothing incredible for such a strong compound. Philosophy says that this saline matter has been accumulating for ages as salt lakes have no outlet; that if they had an outlet, this saline condition would cease to exist. The waters of this lake contain as much salt as it can hold in solution ; to the taste it does not seem to have any other foreign matter, being not at all brackish. The only animal life found in this salt basin is a little insect about as large as a mosquito; this tiny creature appears to be dressed in a fringe of delicate scarlet feathers, and are only observed when there is froth gathered upon the water. There is running upon this lake, a stern wheel steamer, called the "General Garfield;" the accommodations are good and the tourist will find it a pleasant trip to take when on the way to visit the wonders of California.

Persons desiring a bath should provide themselves with a bathing suit before leaving the city. The dresses at the bath houses are left as they have been used by others, so coated with salt that it is quite impossible to get into one, besides most of them are flowing garments, and nothing but tight dresses should be used. Blue drilling overalls, with a cheap cotton or flannel shirt, which one can buy ready made, affords an appropriate outfit. A Mormon patriarch supplied me with this outfit, and I feel prepared to recommend it. I should have lost the opportunity of taking a bath but for this act of generosity on the part of the Mormon, and he was obliged to forego the pleasure of a bath himself until another time, as we all remained in the water until train time.

I thought surely that I had no right to expect to survive this bath of two hours duration, but found it quite impossible to get away from those persistent Mormons. Like the English, the world over, they are bound to have their own way, and control all that is near them; and they will nearly smother one with their officious hospitality. It is the sheer, persistent, selfish will of these people that causes them to hold so many women in that abominable slavery. I have never observed that simple element so strongly marked in any other nationality, except the English The bath did me no injury, however, aside from the fact that I was so exhausted that I did not sit up much of the time upon the following day. There was no lameness or soreness from the unusual exercise, and upon the whole I was benefitted; but staying in the strange element, cutting all manner of physical maneuvers, tired me to such an extent. that one night's rest was not sufficient to recuperate exhausted energies.

It is said that one cannot sink in this water, but I'll assure you that if they cannot swim and get beyond their depth, that they will find themselves reversing positions and attempting to stand upon their heads; as by the laws of gravitation the head is heavier than the feet, the latter will come to the surface like corks. Few of the ladies could swim, and to obviate this difficulty, a wooden frame was brought which was about half the size of a seven by nine window sash; by placing one hand upon this frame and keeping the head out of water, the body would lie upon the surface as if made of wood, and the sensation of being borne upon the water is delightful. Upon leaving the bath I found myself unable to stand without assistance, under the weight of saline matter gathered upon my bathing dress. The weight, of course is not observable while one is in the water, but when walking through the shallow beach to reach the bath house, a person becomes a weighty consideration — one feels as if clothed in a sheet of lead. By the time the dress is removed the skin will be dry, and all that remains to be done, is to take a towel and rub off the dry salt. We are now already pickled, and take the train for the city, more tired if not wiser, than we were in the morning.

I met Judge McKean, and heard from his lips the story of Ann Eliza and the alimony. By the way if it were not for offending some of my handsome gentlemen acquaintances in California, I would pronounce Judge McKean, the best appearing and finest looking man of fifty that I ever met. He is evidently neither saturated with tobacco nor soaked with whisky; his eyes are as clear as the visual organs of a boy sixteen. It sounds very unnatural to speak well of a person while living and I will say no more, but wait patiently. When Judge McKean's decision was announced there was a panic among the bishops and elders, and when Brigham Young declared that he had but one legal wife, there was a panic among the plural edition of wives throughout the whole empire, so much so that those who had sufficient intelligence to comprehend the situation, were perfectly horror stricken at the Prophet's evident cowardice. The miserable old sinner, he ought to die by the violent hand of some woman and not be permitted to live out his days in peace.

THE GOLDEN STATE.

HERE I am in the Golden Land, so well pleased that, like the old Queen of Sheba, I exclaim, "The half has not been told me!" Leaving bleak, cold, windy Chicago, so ill that I could not sit up, I began to mend rapidly as I breathed the invigorating air of the great plains. Arriving here after a most delightful journey of six days, I gained sufficient strength to walk three miles without being unduly fatigued.

Delightful as imagination had pictured the overland route, the reality of the beauty and grandeur of the scenery exceeded expectation. Illimitable plains, lofty, snow-capped mountains, and lovely, fertile valleys succeed each other, ever beautiful and ever varying. Among the mountain passes the snow was very deep, but the snow-sheds prevented it from covering the tracks, so there was no danger. One of the snow-sheds was twenty-eight miles in length. Time seemed long as we passed through it, and we greatly regretted that it hid the mountain view from our sight.

My first impressions of the Golden State are more than fancy had painted them. To me the country appears the most beautiful upon earth. The weather is warm and mild. I am writing with open doors and windows, the bright sun cheering me with its vivifying rays, while I hear the hens cackle as they do at home in early spring (they lay eggs all winter). The birds are singing and building their nests. The grass is six inches high, and the foliage is beautifully green, yet people say the season is unusually backward.

Sacramento Valley is called the Garden of California. Its soil is dark and fertile, and yields large quantities of grain. Plowing and sowing were progressing at an immense rate as we passed through it. The Californians do business on the high-pressure principle, and "push things" in a most wonderful fashion.

The climate of San Jose at this season is delightful. Though rain frequently falls, the showers are always warm, and though *earthquakes* occur often, people tell me they " do not mind 'em but just let *'em quake.*" Yet I fancy they are more courageous *after* than *during* the occurrence. The scenery is grand beyond description, and the soil produces an abundance of " edible things."

The people represent every nationality on the face of the earth, yet they possess that true and frank hospitality which boasts not of its deeds of kindness. They say that nothing would induce them to reside permanently elsewhere, yet, when their " pile " is sufficiently great, they intend to visit the homes of their nativity, which memory still fondly cherishes.

The theory of *woman's rights* meets with much opposition, but the broadest and most catholic altitude is allowed it in practice. Three ladies are practicing medicine here, one of whom has a surgical reputation, and all are prosperous, proving that California flesh is, after all, heir to disease, in spite of the climate. Ladies engage in money-making and business pursuits without attracting the envy, opposition or contempt of the weak-minded of either sex. If woman will but earnestly walk onward in the path of rectitude and duty, success will surely sooner or later crown her efforts.

The weather during the entire month of January has been remarkably lovely, warm and mild, clear and sunny, reminding the tourist of the beautiful Indian Summer at home. The air is cool and exhilarating, producing a stimulating effect upon the nervous system. One experiences a slight stinging sensation in lips, tongue and extremities, like reaction of cold, but as the weather has not been at all cold, scarcely chilly, it must be produced by the warm sunshine succeeding the cool, bracing morning air. The atmosphere possesses certain properties which render the invalid wakeful, and it becomes necessary to coax and pet old Somnus ere he will yield his soothing and refreshing embrace.

The soil is as rich and dark-colored as that of Wisconsin, and is equally as fertile and productive in wheat and other cereals, yielding a greater variety of fruits, far surpassing those of that State in quality as well as quantity. Wheat is the great staple. It is now all sown. The farmers in this vicinity are somewhat anxious about this crop, owing to a deficiency of the usual rains, and if the wheat does not attain a certain growth before March, fears are entertained that the crop may prove a failure. Potatoes are not successfully grown in this otherwise productive valley, their growth being so rank that they are fibrous and watery, though in the mountain valleys they are cultivated as well as in any country in the world, Erin not excepted. The native shrubbery and the manner of arranging gardens reminds one of the Southern States.

The city is supplied by Artesian wells and a pure mountain stream of soft water in the neighborhood. Windmill is the motive power employed for all purposes of irrigation. To a stranger they form a quaint addition to the California landscape as they pump the water for moistening and fertilizing hundreds of thousands of otherwise arid and useless acres.

The almond tree belongs to the peach family. It is now in full bloom. The flowers are very beautiful, possessing the delicate tints of the peach blossom. Almonds grown here are remarkably fine, and peanuts of a superior variety are abundantly produced.

Society in newly-settled countries is always mixed. Almost every nation of the habitable earth has its representatives. While some are uncongenial, yet, one meets with many frank, intelligent and hospitable people. As to dress, every mode is fashionable, the latest Paris styles not excepted. People dress just as they choose, without attracting attention, though I must confess that long, swallow-tail coats do appear *mal-a-propos* to the fast Chicagoan, accustomed to the "cur"-tailed business suit. Neither very light summer nor heavy winter garments are required, moderately warm clothing being suitable the whole year.

Californians have a pet earthquake theory. They declare that *their* earthquakes are not volcanic, but entirely atmospheric. As thunder and lightning do not exist they argue that the earthquake is an atmospherical method of purifying the air, and they furthermore assert that since 1812 but few lives have been lost on the entire Pacific Coast, and that thunder and lightning, winds and violent storms cause greater destruction to life and property in the other States than the earthquakes of the Pacific Slope.

Apparently there is little fear of earthquakes, yet the buildings are constructed to guard against these phenomena. They are built of wood, generally low, are one story high, broad on the ground, and surrounded with piazzas. The best recommendation for a house is that it is "earthquake-proof." There are many handsome blocks in San Jose. The roads are hard, smooth and clean, rendering the drives most delightful.

SAN JOSE IN JUNE.

THE floral wealth of San Jose is at this season abundant beyond description. Though climbing plants and several varieties of vines were green all winter, they are of a brighter hue now. The few roses which gladdened us in January and February are succeeded by a progeny as numerous, as ever-varying and beautiful. Double purple violets, hidden beneath the dark green foliage, perfume the air. Large gray pansies, fragrant carnations, myrtle blossoms, and the numerous varieties of bridal wreath and spirea, with drooping limbs studded with clusters of infinitessimal roses of snowy whiteness greet one in every direction, producing feelings of gratitude to the Great Creator that He has thus beautified and adorned bounteous Mother Earth.

Oranges are not cultivated in this valley, though all fruits, such as peaches, apricots, almonds, etc., are grown in abundance with little labor. The grapes are exceedingly heavy. They are Fenian green now, and as the season advances they will receive darker hues, until, like humanity, they become sear and yellow with age. Wheat is the principal cereal, and is extensively cultivated, producing flour of a superfine quality. The mountains, extending from east to west, form one unbroken chain, while the northern and southern horizon is bounded by hills and table-lands. The mountains are covered with an emerald carpet, and the scrub oaks on their heights attest their sterility, while clear, silvery clouds crown their lofty peaks like a halo.

The table-lands are luxuriant with grain fields and meadows, and the white farm-house upon the distant hill, surrounded by its peach orchard, present a lovely landscape to the beholder—a landscape of mountains, hills, valley and table-land, sterility and fertility—like the characteristics of life. Horrible tales of devouring lions and panthers are rehearsed to us, now and then, but as we have seen no trace of either animal we are inclined to think that the tales are mythical.

FIRST IMPRESSIONS OF A CALIFORNIA EARTHQUAKE.

IN February, at noon-day, I experienced my first introduction to a shock of California earthquake. I had been out enjoying my customary morning promenade, the weather being mild and balmy as usual, and the face of nature appeared serene. On entering my room, as I was removing my bonnet and shawl, the building suddenly began to rock, and the blinds shook and swayed to and fro just like a steamer getting under way. I caught hold of a table and steadied myself to regain my equilibrium. I for a moment imagined that I had just embarked at San Francisco, and had taken passage for the Sandwich Islands. Another moment's reflection, however, gave me to understand that instead of being on the "briny deep," I was upon *terra firma*, and that the rocking sensation was my first introduction, in California vulgate, to a "Quake." Scarcely had I regained my position ere the rocking and trembling ceased, and, strange to say, I was not in the least alarmed. Going towards the door I met my next door neighbor with a composed smile, as if "Quakes" were already familiar things. She was greatly frightened, and regarding my composure as forced, remarked, "They who know nothing, fear nothing." If this be true, when I know more I will fear more.

Occupying the second story of a fine building, my first impulse after the shake was over was to look about for damages. In my room the plastered walls were somewhat crushed, but that was all. Going to the window to see what the people in the street were doing, I observed that the people were a trifle agitated, and the windows on the opposite side of the street were filled with eager and anxious faces, looking in the same direction, probably for the same purpose.

The greatest and only real danger resulting from these phenomena is caused by crowds of people rushing hurriedly into the streets, and being hurt by falling chimneys, and other missiles. I am told that all loss of life on the Pacific has resulted from fearful stampedes of children from the public schools, or crowds of people tumbling and trampling and jostling each other in the first moments of alarm.

If, as Holland says, "All common good has common price," the price of living in this country, as far as my experience goes, is rather the fear than the result of earthquakes. As there are neither violent winds or storms, thunder or lightning, whirlwinds or simoons, nature purifies the elements by shakes and quakes, and all fears rest in the fact that no one knows how hard it may shake before the quake is over.

In a former chapter I spoke of windmills. They are a most interesting and pleasant institution of this country, and as reliable as sunrise and sunset. The winds blow with great regularity every day, from the South in winter and from the North in summer. Thus, windmills are a never-failing source of irrigation. It is a pleasing sight to view their giant arms tossed about by balmy breezes, doing a giant's work, pumping the water into troughs, from which it is then guided by hose in every required direction.

The weather during February was charming— mild and spring-like, with only one wintry day, and that a very pleasant one to a Northerner.

SANTA CLARA.

THIS old Spanish town is so near San Jose that it may properly be called one of its environs. Though a Western spirit of progress is here and there visible, animating the natural indolence of her inhabitants, the old, unprogressive Spanish element, with its adherence to and veneration for all that has been, is as yet the prevailing one might say the dominant spirit. Its climate is semi-tropical, and owing to the near proximity of the Pacific is subject to the bracing ocean breezes, which in a measure counteract the debility consequent upon all warm climates, and though therefore very mild and agreeable, it fails to produce that stimulating oxygen so necessary to persons who were born and reared in more northerly latitudes. All productions indiginous to the Temperate zones, and almost all those of the Tropics, flourish luxuriantly. Extensive orchards, yielding almost every variety of fruit known to the Temperate and Tropical zones, and well cultivated kitchen gardens give evidence that the gastronomic tastes and wants of the people of this community are not neglected.

OVER THE MOUNTAINS TO SANTA CRUZ.

LEAVING San Jose southwestward for Santa Cruz, we make our transit by means of an old-fashioned conservative stage coach, which when one is not in a hurry, and the weather is dry, mild and balmy, and the road diversified by hill and valley, mountains and streams, is a very agreeable way of travel. This valley is one of the most fertile in California, and unsurpassed in picturesque scenery, with the exception of the Yosemite. In the full meridian of spring Nature assumes her most attractive garb. The wheat fields of the valleys and foot-hills give promise of a fair harvest, while the foliage of the hills and mountains is yet fresh and green, and brilliant-hued wild flowers dot the level fields. Indeed, every variety of scenery greets the tourist's eye.

The fertile foot-hills furnish pasturage for immense herds of cattle, sheep and goats. The undulating slopes of the hills are covered with brush and small timber, and then the mountain pass, with its deep ravines, its yawning precipices and gigantic trees, which, while they inspire the soul with the grandeur of the mighty works of the Great Creator, also produce the painful effect of fear upon the nerves of the timid traveler. The mountain gorges are often five hundred feet in depth, while projecting rocks, with mammoth trees growing from them, and bending over the precipice, as if about to fall, meet one at every turn of a curve. Now and then we pass over a plateau of table-land in a very high state of cultivation. The air ascending the mountains is bracing and delightfully fragrant with the perfume of wild flowers and new mown hay.

The mountain stage drivers are peculiar characters, and deserve a passing notice. They are veterans of their occupation, having driven for years on the same route. In California vulgate, they never get foggy—which means that they are temperate—an unusual recommendation in this country. They are very trusty, possessing an accurate knowledge of every step of the hazardous way, and know something of interest about every spot. No smoking is allowed either inside or outside the stage, so that ladies can ride outside if they choose and obtain a perfect view of the natural scenery, a privilege of which many avail themselves. The stages are drawn by six horses, which are relieved every ten miles. The mountain ascent is very laborious and is slowly made, but the descent is rapid.

The mountain streams are well filled with trout, and fishing parties are quite fashionable in the vicinity of the trout streams—we ladies taking particular delight in following this indolently pleasurable pursuit of Isaac Walton—and as we return with long strings well-filled with the speckled shiners and enjoy the delicious repast they afford, we feel well repaid for the sport by which we captured the delicious specimens of the finny tribe.

Midway between San Jose and Santa Cruz there is a place of entertainment for man and beast, kept like the old-fashioned country taverns of the East. Here, while we sumptuously fared, we were forcibly reminded of Yankee Land. Reminiscences of home are ever pleasurable to the sojourner in a strange land, particularly when they appear in the form of a well-cooked dinner, with the addition of a plate of well-browned trout.

The descriptions by travelers of the mammoth trees of California are no exaggeration. The weeping willow grows to such an immense circumference that one can drive a span of horses and wagon beneath the shade of its gracefully drooping branches. The redwood trees attain such a gigantic size that our tallest oaks are mere pygmies in comparison, and the fir trees grow straight as reeds, and so very tall that one would suppose they intended to find their level with the highest mountain tops.

The City of Santa Cruz, or Holy Cross, is delightfully situated upon the sea, at a distance of half a mile from the bay of Monterey, and thirty-five miles southwest of San Jose. It is quite a place of resort, as it possesses a fine beach. Its bathing facilities are hardly equal to those of Newport.

Its streets are fine and cleanly, and its hotels

commodious. Its stores are very countrified, dealing in goods of every description, from shawls to codfish. It possesses some manufactures and considerable commerce. The flowing wells are a great curiosity. They are bored like Artesian wells, often two hundred feet deep, and the water gushes and boils up and runs over, yielding an abundant and constant supply.

Each distinctive feature of farming is carried on as a separate business here. One man devotes his entire time and means to the culture of grain, another to vegetables, a third cultivates grapes, a fourth fruits, a fifth cattle, etc. Owing to the necessity of irrigation and the variety of the soil and climate this becomes a necessity, and when failure occurs it becomes a very disastrous one. It is an easy matter to make a livelihood in California, but as difficult to amass a fortune as in other countries.

JUNE WEATHER AND TRADE WINDS.

OUR June weather has been very warm during the day, but the heat is greatly mitigated towards its close by the trade winds, which never fail to blow regularly from the North every afternoon, and render our evenings and nights cool and enjoyable. One can always sleep well in this climate—a blessing which nervous patients who have suffered from the want of weary nature's sweet restorer can fully appreciate. Linens, lawns, muslins, organdies, and in fact summer clothing of any description can be worn only during the middle of the day. As soon as the trade winds arise the atmosphere becomes so cool that heavy clothing, like broadcloths, merinos, and even furs are not only comfortable but necessary to prevent taking cold. The cool evenings and nights, and the good, healthful sleep are so refreshing that the heat of noon-day does not produce the debility of other warm climates. In this respect the Pacific Coast has greatly the advantage over the Central and South Atlantic Coast.

Grapes are growing finely; the clusters are round and full, and give promise of an abundant harvest. Their roots strike so deep into the earth that the drought does not affect them; in fact, dry weather is beneficial to grapes, rendering them sweeter and freer from rust and mildew. Raisins of excellent flavor and superior quality are extensively produced. Much suffering is caused by the dust, though perhaps not more than in other localities, where no rain has fallen for a long period of time.

The flowing wells have proved as great a blessing as the water which gushed from the desert rock was to the thirsty Israelites. They continue to gush and bubble and give forth their inestimable wealth of fresh, sweet, pure water in abundance, without a thought of the drought, whose disastrous effects are so manifest to those who are deprived of them. Little pools of water collect about the wells, which the feathered tribe scent from afar, and they come hither in myriads to wet their thirsty little beaks and bathe and flap their wings in the limpid stream. Then they perch themselves among the boughs of our shade trees and pour forth their songs of thanksgiving, to which it is most pleasurable to listen.

The aboriginal settlers were either Spanish or French, and these have become so mixed with the native Indian element that it is difficult to trace distinct types of either nationality. They are uneducated, particularly the women, and their ignorance reacts on all. They speak no language correctly or purely, but a jargon of all. The tourist who remarked that upon inquiring the nationality of a lady and received the reply "Me no mucho Francaise, Englise, you bet" describes their language correctly. Still, one recognizes the French by their politeness, their neatness of dress—whatever their surroundings—their sociability, and their general superiority to the Spaniards, or old Californians, as they are termed. These are not particularly neat, having a strong penchant for oils, Cayenne pepper, hard boiled eggs and plenty of garlic.

The ladies wear shawls upon their heads, are small in stature, and either grow to an enormous embonpoint or wither and dry up until they resemble Egyptian mummies. They are exceedingly conservative, don't approve of schools, and do just as their grand-parents and great grand-parents did before them, from father Noah down, the example of which venerable patriarch they religiously imitate by making free use of the fermented juice of the grape, with the addition thereto of corn-juice in the form of whiskey and other alcoholic beverages. They generally dislike progress and the Yankees, and sell their estates and emigrate to Mexico.

Lord Macaulay has termed the religion of the old Californians, "That fascinating superstition which shall nevertheless be the prevailing faith when the tourist shall sketch the ruins of Westminster Abbey from a broken arch of London Bridge." Should this prophecy prove true of London, it will never apply to California, for progressive ideas are storming the battlements of ancient prejudice and superstition, and even the Catholic church cannot restrain the onward march. The

French do not permit their religious scruples to interfere with their sociability or their neighborly kindness; but it is different with the Spaniards who are ultra High Church; they believe that none can obtain an immortal Elysium but themselves, and fear contamination from other influences; hence they are jealous and taciturn, and liberal Christians assert that the greater their ignorance the greater their faith—but these are heretical views, diametrically opposite to orthodox belief, and must be judged accordingly.

The greatest drawback is the land monopoly. The farmers are buying up and holding thousands of acres of the most valuable public lands, and holding them so high that poor men cannot purchase cheap homes. These speculators keep the country from improving as fast as it would if the poor man were not thus fettered.

SUMMER CLIMATE IN SAN JOSE.

THE summer climate here has been extremely hot and dry during the past season; but one little shower of rain fell in the latter part of July, and though the ocean breezes cooled the atmosphere at the close of day and at night, and were somewhat refreshing, they failed to alleviate the weariness and lassitude caused by the day's heat, or to cure the desire to postpone all physical and mental labor till the morrow, and when the morrow came, to postpone it till cooler weather. The oldest settlers aver that the past summer has been an unusually hot one, and though that may be, still the climate of the heated term loses its usual brain and muscle stimulating properties, unless it be that what is brain stimulating is also brain trying, and that the system, when reaction occurs, is left in a more debilitated condition than if the stimulant had not been employed.

Threshing grain is carried on as extensively and expeditiously as everything else in this country. Several threshing machines, accompanied by the usual number of operatives or "hands" surround the mammoth grain stacks and commence work, resting only long enough to "take in food" for man and beast. At night the men sleep in the field in near proximity to the stacks, with no other bed than the bare ground and a single blanket. As the air is warm, perfectly free from damps and dews, and not the least danger of a shower, they sleep soundly until sunrise, when work begins again, and continues uninterruptedly until all is completed.

Grasses become sere and dry in midsummer, one might say almost from the effects of heat, and he who does not understand the order of things in this climate would pronounce them burnt and worthless; nevertheless, cattle eat, live and thrive upon them, growing fat and sleek as the season advances. Some species of California grasses produce small burrs, which fall upon and cover the ground when ripe. These are nutritive for cattle, and are eaten with avidity by them.

The people enjoy summer fruits of almost every variety and climate. Cherries, plums, apricots, and peaches. There are two crops of strawberries. Berries of every variety abound in their season. Elderberries are as large as good sized peas, and covered with a white mist, giving them the appearance of sugar-coated pills. Grapes are plentiful, large, sweet and luscious, some of the clusters almost equaling in size and plumpness, the pictured representations of those famous bunches found in the Promised Land by the spies of the Children of Israel, which were wont to make our mouth water in early childhood, as we beheld them suspended from a pole and borne upon the brawny shoulders of the fault-finding Jews.

The native wines are very sweet, the warm, dry weather being highly adapted to the growth and development of the grapes. As usual, the winemakers claim that their wines are not intoxicating. They certainly taste very sweet and palatable, and if never drank to excess might not injure the cause of temperance—but, judging from what we have seen we incline to the contrary opinion. Some large varieties of grapes produce raisins equal to the best imported Malagas, particularly those cultivated amid the sheltered valleys and foothills.

SAN FRANCISCO.

SAN FRANCISCO, to a stranger from the Prairie Land, accustomed to the level, monotonous scenery of home, is most delightfully situated. Portions of the city, being built upon picturesque hills, which, like those of St. Paul, Minnesota, have not been graded down to make level streets, but left in their natural beauty, present an undulating and pleasing prospect to an admirer of varied scenery. These elevations afford excellent views of the city, the bay, crowded with shipping, and the Golden Gate, with its open welcome to the sea.

The churches have fewer and less elevated steeples than those of the Eastern cities; probably they are constructed with reference to earthquakes, which, though claimed by scientific men to be atmospheric instead of volcanic, nevertheless cause more damage to lofty than lower structures. The business houses are large and spacious, for the Californians like plenty of room, and that as near *terra firma* as possible. The merchants are particularly fond of fresh air and sunshine, and many of them transact their business upon the sidewalk. The scene from the bay is enchanting to a lover of variety. Steamers are leaving for Panama and other points, crowded with passengers who are flirting adieus with their handkerchiefs to friends on shore. A schooner, too heavily or unevenly laden with baled hay has upset, scattering her cargo in every direction upon the blue waters, the hay following the current and sailing towards the Pacific. White barges and water craft of every description are being loaded and unloaded by people of every hue and nationality.

As for the autumn climate of this city, whatever it may be at other seasons, it is anything but salubrious or agreeable to pulmonary or bronchial invalids, and the sooner they make their exit from San Francisco, the better it will be for their coughs and colds. Fogs are frequent, are very heavy, and have an inflammatory effect upon throat, lungs, eyes and nose.

The climate of San Francisco, according to the testimony of their meteorologists, is unlike that of any other city in the world. It has essentially two climates, and there is a constant conflict between the land and sea temperature for supremacy. The ocean breeze partakes of the temperature of the Pacific, which is about fifty-three degrees Fahrenheit the whole year. From the Coast Range of mountains, near the Golden Gate, there is a current of cool, damp air, of the same temperature as the ocean, laden with misty clouds, which linger near the base of the hills and penetrate the valleys around San Francisco Bay.

The land temperature is as nearly opposite to that of the ocean as possible. It is generally hot and dry, and the two climates, acting upon each other produce one which has no parallel anywhere. The extensive territory lying about the bay is within scope of these two climates, and subject to their joint influence. Though neither very warm nor very cold, and quite stimulating to mental and physical energies, it is nevertheless not the perfectly healthful climate which invalids from the Atlantic States come in search of. One chills so easily, and there are so many weather changes that it is almost impossible to dress properly to meet them. Colds and catarrh are prevalent, and pocket handkerchiefs, cough drops, bronchial troches, and every species of patent medicine advertised for these afflictions are in active and constant demand.

The face of Nature here during the last days of November is exceedingly charming. Scarcely a more beautiful sight can be imagined than the sudden, cheerful change presented by the surrounding hills after the first showers. These hills are treeless, and their sharp peaks and deep gullied sides are covered with a carpet of deep, velvety green, which is their winter garb. Plants and flowers flourish finely in the open air, as no irrigation is now needed to keep them in full growth and bloom. Ornamental plants grow to a size unknown in Eastern cities. The cactus variety attains a gigantic size, while the fuchsias are ten or twelve feet in height, and bloom profusely throughout the entire winter in the open air.

Geraniums of every variety, heliotropes, oleanders—in fact all our Eastern hot-house plants find their native and congenial climate here.

San Francisco possesses many fine public buildings. Among these is the Orphan Asylum, which looms up from one of her hills like an ancient feudal castle, its substantial stone walls being covered with ivy and clambering vines, while the sloping hill-sides descending from it are green with the verdure of grass and shrubbery. Her churches, school-buildings and private dwellings are not excelled in architectural beauty or convenience and adaptability by those of her sister cities in the East.

The liquor traffic is here as with the whole nation, the most money-making pursuit, and whisky and stimulating and intoxicating beverages of every description are the curse of this coast. Red noses, bleared eyes, foul breaths, and all the train of physical and mental evils which follow the daily use of alcoholic beverages are everywhere apparent. The native born children have a fine physical development, and were it not for the inheritance of intemperance might, in a few generations, attain mankind's primitive perfection in health and longevity.

San Francisco possesses many valuable manufactories. The manufacture of silver plate of chaste and elaborate designs and excellent quality is largely carried on. Woolen blankets, of soft, fleecy texture, and shawls, gloves and hose are produced in such abundance as to supply the entire home market. There is great jealousy of Eastern manufacturers who send their productions here to find a market, and many consider the Pacific Railroad as a detriment, since foreign manufacturers can compete with and destroy the profits of home industry in a greater degree than when commerce was entirely carried on by water. Silk culture is constantly developing, and is quite profitable to the producer. The cocoons are of a much finer quality than those of Japan and China, and though silk is not successfully manufactured here, the cocoons find a ready market in France and Italy.

THE VERNAL SEASON ON THE PACIFIC COAST.

TO Northern and Eastern sojourners the vernal season here, in the metropolis of the Pacific Coast, is so far advanced that spring appears lost in the gorgeous bloom of mid-summer. The reign of flowers is fully upon us, and many of the earlier varieties of annual roses have passed their season and are covering the ground with their faded leaves, while the later varieties and the perpetual bloomers perfume the air and beautify the landscape. Bouquets, composed of all the more hardy roses, camelias and japonicas, intermingled with fuchsias and less choice flowers are abundant and decorate stores, churches and homes. Oranges and the fruits of the season are coming into market too, as well as an endless variety of vegetables.

The Chinese are very successful in the cultivation of the latter—as well as all manner of horticultural and agricultural productions. They possess the faculty of making a few acres yield as much as an American would grow on three times the quantity of land. Every inch of ground is cultivated, and their economy is beyond everything. All their vegetables are brought to market by means of the neck yoke.

The Chinese constitute one of the peculiar institutions of the Pacific Coast, as do the negroes of the Southern States. It is curious to watch them in their labors, and especially in their homes, which for dense population in limited space may well be compared to ant-hills. Their unlimited perseverance makes them successful in whatever they undertake.

Upon the long flats extending along the Oakland and Alameda shores the Chinamen have extensive fisheries, and when they cast their nets amid the shoals of smelt and herring which abound here at high water, they capture myriads of these shiners with the same facility, ease and success as appear to crown all their efforts. When their boats are filled with glittering heaps of fishes, then begins the work of cleaning, drying and packing; while so engaged, the Chinaman lightens his toil by a low, guttural song, which evidently cheers him and fills his soul with pleasing dreams of his flowery home, though to Christian ears the noise he makes is not only devoid of melody, but perfectly heathenish.

In the mines, the Chinese work steadily and faithfully, and where this industry is extensively carried on they are more reliable than miners of European nationality. They have many curious ceremonies and religious rites. Although all those who have the means are buried in the land of their nativity, many die here who are too poor, or have no friends to send their remains thither. These have a burial place provided for them in San Francisco, to which all orthodox Chinamen make a semi-annual pilgrimage, for the purpose of placing rice and other provisions upon the graves of those of their countrymen who are forced to sleep their last sleep in the land of the barbarians.

They then bless or charm numerous pieces of

paper, tear these into small bits, and scatter them to the four points of the compass—a ceremony which they believe exorcises and banishes evil spirits, and prevents them from disturbing the repose of their deceased friends. Heathen though they are, they are by no means averse or indifferent to the teachings of Christianity. Several Protestant denominations have been very successful in the work of proselyting.

The ignorance, immorality and servility of the women of China is the main obstacle to the elevation of the Chinese as a people. Like the Mohammedan nations of the East, and all heathen and barbarous people, they believe women to be a lower order of beings, without souls, to whom Paradise will be denied hereafter, and whose sole earthly mission is to minister to man and to serve him. For ages this slavery has existed, and the Chinawoman is as perfectly satisfied with her condition as Mesdames Sherman and Dahlgren and the Massachusetts protestors against woman suffrage. Like these respected ladies, they regard the woman who is dissatisfied with her condition as a most horrible and unnatural monstrosity, and the very few heroines that China has produced are held up to posterity as models of sin and inspirations of the spirit of evil. Polygamy is universal, and the highest ambition of woman is to be a meek and humble consort to her husband, who is her lord and master.

Manufactures are being constantly encouraged and developed in San Francisco. Blankets and woolen cloths are woven here which cannot be excelled in any portion of the world. The manufacture of silk is not yet in a flourishing condition, owing to want of capital and to the great demand for cocoons for exportation. Several glove factories are prosperous and promise to supply not only the home market, but portions of South America, the Pacific Coast States, and the Territories. Buckskins and dog-skins are commonly used, the former for working gloves and the latter for riding and driving gloves. The buckskins are sold in the markets in large quantities by hunters and trappers, and are tanned at the different tanneries in the vicinity of the city. Woolen gloves of a very superior quality and finish are extensively manufactured for Montana and the more Northern countries. Kid glove making will become profitable in time, when more attention is given to the rearing of goats; as yet, many so called kid gloves are made of lamb, squirrel, and even cat-skins. The sewing of gloves is generally done by women, many of whom work at their homes as in the factories.

San Francisco is a city that awakens the sympathies of the philanthropist and humanitarian more fully than any other of its size and natural advantages. The natural influx of strangers from all parts of the earth, and the numberless disappointed ones who came hither with golden dreams which have never been realized, the commingling of many incongruous elements, the dearth of labor and the distress consequent thereon—all touch the sympathetic heart.

THE SAN JOAQUIN RIVER.

THE waters of the San Joaquin (pronounced by the natives San Waukeen) River, are dark and muddy with the soil which is swept into them from the mining regions in the mountains. The San Joaquin Valley is a great grain producing district. Thousands of tons of wheat are awaiting shipment, the home market being glutted with breadstuffs of every kind. Plums, figs, almonds and grapes grow abundantly. The latter are pruned until they appear as though nothing remained but the roots and a branch or two, yet they very soon grow to vines and yield an abundant harvest.

Such vegetables as beets and carrots grow to an enormous size—the former sometimes weighing fifty pounds; they are unfit to eat and are fed to cattle. A great profusion of wild flowers bloom around the base of the mountains; among these the yellow violet, with a dark center, and the California poppy are most numerous; the latter is very poisonous, and the cattle avoid it with that brute instinct which teaches them its dangerous properties.

The experiment of importing Cashmere goats promises to become a success in this valley. The goats soon become acclimated, and will eventually prove very profitable to their owners. Great herds of cattle and immense flocks of sheep are to be found on the fine pasturage upon the sunny slopes of the hills and in the mountain valleys; the sheep are sometimes watched by a shepherd, who appears to the tourist the very picture of indolent repose; as we saw one reclining lazily upon a mossy bank, resting his right arm upon his crook, we recalled to mind a libelous anecdote of one of his confreres. A traveler among the Alps relates, that during his peregrinations he found a shepherd weeping bitterly, and apparently in great distress; upon inquiring what the trouble was, the shepherd replied that he was very hungry. "Well, get up, my good friend—come with me, and I will attend to your necessities," said the traveler. "Oh, good sir, if I chose to get up I could get my own dinner, which is in that basket, hanging on yonder tree; if you wish to do a kind act, please bring it to me, for I have not the energy to fetch it myself," replied the shepherd. "Well, friend," said the traveler, "if you are too lazy to get up, why then starve."

The sagacious instinct of the shepherd dog is truly wonderful; the utmost reliance can be placed upon him, for he never neglects his trust—always keeping the sheep within a certain limit, and guarding them from wolves and other dangers; he certainly deserves eulogism, for however indolent his master may be, he is ever on the alert, and though he may suffer the pangs of hunger, he has never been known to attack, kill or eat a sheep.

The location of Sacramento renders it unhealthy and subject to agues, fevers, and all diseases of a malarious nature; the sudden melting of the mountain snow swells the river to such an extent that the city and surrounding country are often inundated, producing great destruction to life and property—and additional malaria is caused by the receding of the waters. Notwithstanding these natural disadvantages, Sacramento is steadily improving; many buildings are in process of construction, some of which are fine palatial structures, but the greatest number are modest, genteel little cottages, adapted to the wants of families who desire to live pleasantly and keep out of debt —on a small income.

At the State House we endeavored to take an inventory of a small mountain of whiskey, wine and beer bottles and oyster shells—by which it was surrounded, but our mathematics failed, and we gave up the attempt in despair. Won't we women have a time cleaning these Augean stables of wine, whiskey and beer bottles, cigar stumps, broken pipes, tobacco juice, etc. when *we* vote and legislate. It's a fearful responsibility, O California legislators, and though we assume it with prayerful fear and trembling, we shall not hesitate to do our duty when the hour arrives.

One of the features of Sacramento is her restaurants. They are numerous, clean and well kept. Many travelers, and even resident families, procure their meals here, as in Paris, Berlin, and the European capitols. A masculine waiter receives $40 per month and expenses, while the female waiter, for doing exactly the same work, and doing it with greater despatch and more adaptability, receives $20. What a comment upon the injustice practiced by the voting towards the nonvoting citizen!

But "for the desert the fountain is springing," as the Legislature has made important changes in respect to the rights of women. It is now provided that the earnings of the wife shall not be liable for the debts of the husband; that the earnings and accumulations of the wife and her minor children, living with or being in her custody, if the wife be living separate or apart from her husband, shall be the separate property of the wife, and that the wife, if living separate or apart from her husband, shall have the exclusive use and control of her separate property, may sue and be sued, without joining or being joined by her husband, and may avail herself of and be subject to all legal process in all actions, including actions concerning her real estate.

GILROY.

GILROY is laid out like Superior City and McGregor, Iowa—that is, one continuous and exceedingly long street, upon which all the business houses, and the most prominent private dwellings are located. For a pioneer Western town it strikes the stranger as a marvel of neatness; its buildings are large and capacious, occupying much space upon the ground, and are nearly all one story in height, to render them less liable to fall from earthquakes.

California develops precocious growth in all things–vegetables, fruit, trees, cities and children. This rapid growth exhausts vitality and leads to early decay, and often premature death. Capacious stores, whose thick Venetian shades close out the cheerful light of our bright skies, attract many customers, and looking at the signs above their doors we read, "Sample Rooms," and the nature of the samples sold there is made manifest to the stranger by the red noses and bleared eyes of the numerous customers who patronize these "sample rooms," which, like all the drinking saloons of California and the entire West, do a flourishing business, and in a measure account for much of the depression evident in the useful and happier vocations of life, since they lure their patrons to temptation and ruin, and unfit them for every good and noble purpose.

It is indeed pleasurable to turn from these well patronized whiskey shops and their degenerate patrons, to the lovely natural surroundings of the town. Ranges of majestic hills raise their misty summits from all points of the compass, encircling it like a beautiful verdure-crowned fortification of nature. Spring is far advanced, plowing and planting nearly over, and the hopes of a remunerative harvest are thus far excellent.

Fourteen miles from here are located the Gilroy Hot Springs, celebrated in the State for their medicinal properties. They are sulphuric, somewhat resembling the Warm Springs, of Litte Rock, Arkansas, and are very efficacious for rheumatic diseases, coughs, colds and liver disorders; they are much frequented by invalids from this and neighboring States, as Gilroy is easily reached by railway, and the last fourteen miles are accomplished by stages, which run regularly twice a week.

This vicinity is largely settled by people from the South Atlantic and Gulf States, with an intermixture of a "right smart sprinkling" of enterprising Yankees, and consequently the appearance of Gilroy is more pleasing and progressive than that of the neighboring Spanish towns. The Yankee element, like the English language, having absorbed all others, until the individual identity of each is lost—the good and evil of both, like tares and wheat, continue to grow together. Thus, an enterprising weekly newspaper is published here, and churches and rooster fights are both well patronized on Sundays, and schools and drinking-saloons on week days. Vice and immorality, as in older communities, rear their destroying heads amid virtue and purity. The climate is very fine, never extremely warm or severely cold, with a dry, bracing air, clear, sunny skies, and invigorating sea and mountain breezes.

LOS ANGELES.

LOS ANGELES, owing to its inland situation, presents an aspect of isolation to the tourist who visits it for the first time. It is located twenty miles from San Pedro Bay, an inlet of the Pacific, with which it is connected by a railroad, which is the only one in the State, at present, south of Santa Clara county. The coast range of mountains, in proximity to the Pacific, extends through the entire length of Los Angeles county in a northwestern and southeastern direction. The city itself is situated in an arid, alkaline valley, clothed with a very sparse vegetation between it and San Pedro Bay, which is the case, with the exception of small, fertile tracts, in the entire surrounding country.

This portion of Southern California corresponds

in climate to that of the south shore of Europe, from the Bosphorus to Gibraltar. In clearness of sky, in mildness and equality of temperature, it is said to surpass the climate of the Italian and Spanish coasts, and those whose heaven is always farther West, ever beyond the pale of advanced civilization, pronounce it much more attractive. The mountain summits are covered with snow, consequently the wind currents which blow from them are cold, mitigating the natural tropical heat. The influence of the trade winds, inland from the ocean, though they increase the heat of summer and the cold of winter, are obviated by the regular sea breezes, which make the winters warmer and the summers cooler. These varied natural causes produce a really magnificent climate, which may be compared to a constant and beautiful spring.

Notwithstanding that large tracts of country are of an alkaline nature, wholly barren, presenting a white, desolate appearance, as if the earth had been thickly dusted with flour, there are other more fertile portions, which, though quite as arid in appearance, partake of the sandy qualities of the soil of Florida and the coast districts of the West Indies. These produce the fruits of the tropical and semi-tropical climates in great abundance. Oranges and raisins are the principal productions.

Orange culture is a leading branch of industry. The trees flourish in the open air like common orchard trees of the North, and the fruit ripens from December to May, at a time when there are few oranges from the Haiwaiian or adjacent islands in the California markets. Healthy trees in full bearing produce a thousand or more oranges a year, whose marketable value is estimated at from two to five dollars per hundred. The trees do not come to full maturity before they are ten years old, and will not thrive in arid soil without irrigation.

There are many orange nurseries in this vicinity, where hundreds of thousands of young trees are sown and then grafted before being transplanted into orchards. The orange tree is not as hardy as is generally supposed, at least not in this country, where it is not indigenous, but imported, though with careful culture it is becoming acclimated. Many perish in transplanting, and in the nurseries they are subject to the attacks of gophers, which destroy them, and a bug called the orange aphis, which injures the leaves, rendering the trees barren, and causing them to perish. No method of killing this insect, or averting its destroying ravages has as yet been discovered; like the cut-worm of northern climes, it comes, commits its work of devastation and then disappears without any known cause. Lemons, sweet and sour limes, flourish, and produce abundantly. Their culture is similar to the orange and they are subject to the same diseases and destroying influences.

Next to orange culture, the cultivation of the grape is the leading agricultural industry of Los Angeles county. The production of wines and brandies amounts to thousands of gallons, and great quantities of fresh grapes are used in home consumption and for exportation. The Tokay and Muscat wines are produced superior to those in Europe, while Port, Burgundy, Hock, Claret and Champagne are said to be (by epicurean drinkers), equal to the best vintages of France and the Rhine valley. The Malaga grape yields large, fine raisins, which command a ready market and remunerative prices. The fig tree thrives and yields abundantly in those situations which are on a level with the sea and exempt from the keen ocean breezes. Dates, palms, olives, English walnuts, almonds and peanuts thrive with little care and well repay the laborer for their cultivation. North of this city the country is unsettled and uncultivated, and where alkali lands do not exist, is well adapted to grazing purposes, though its liability to drought is a great drawback.

The population, like that of all South California, is greatly mixed. Many nationalities and people find representatives here. Our Southern ex-slaveholding, aristocratic element, who believe that advanced civilization can only exist where the masses are illiterate, and hence subservient to the educated few, whose mission it is to be the governing and thinking power as is theirs to be the muscular and laboring power, and who, like the old Bourbons, learn nothing and forget nothing, have taken refuge here, where both climate and surroundings are congenial. Among them are many professional men, particularly lawyers. There are Germans from the Rhine land who cultivate the grape; Italians and French engage in silk culture; conservative Spaniards whose complexions and exteriors resemble the oil, the olives and the garlic of which they are so fond, and who have progressed sufficiently to substitute cock fights for the famous bull fights which were the delight of their chivalrous ancestors; plodding, blinking, almond-eyed Chinamen, who engage in any and every pursuit, always useful and moderately successful in whatever they undertake; Mexicans, in whom the evil propensities of Spaniard and Indian progenitors are inherent; Jews, Englishmen and Irishmen, Digger Indians, and a very small proportion of smart unadulterated Yankees from "daown East," who as yet wield but little influence among a population of five thousand souls, composed of so many races and such commingling of nationalities. Thieves, vagabonds, and criminals from the "Upper Country," as the territory of the North is called, infest a rendezvous in the mountain districts, and often make their way hither on their route to Mexico, which is their terrestrial paradise. In consequence of their lawless depredations, a vigilance committee has been organized, composed of some of the leading citizens who occasionally hang a desperado or two on the plazzas or gate posts of the old Spanish adobe houses, which seem especially constructed for that purpose.

Private and public buildings bear the impress of Spanish nationality, being constructed of adobe, in close proximity to each other, with the broad overshadowing piazzas, without which no Spaniard's house is complete, and which are so connected that in the rainy season one can promenade the whole length of a street beneath their shelter. The gates to the courts or outer yards of these buildings are a curiosity, reminding one of the Medieval ages, with their great, ponderous gallows-like frame work, which seem solely constructed for the hanging business. There are some handsome modern buildings, but the general aspect of the city is Spanish. Notwithstanding the delightful climate of this portion of Southern California, with its luscious fruits and abundance and variety of wild game, it has many drawbacks, which serve to intimidate the ardor and peace-loving emigrant. Its isolated situation, with its barren tracts of alkali, whose dust is very injurious to the eyes, its mixed population, the frequency of brawls, street fights and murders, and the insecurity and immorality consequent upon tropical latitudes, its liability to severe droughts, are all powerful causes which will operate against the future development of this land of smiling skies, whose olives and vines are emblematical of a people who have never attained a high or permanent degree of civilization and enlightenment.

PETALUMA.

THE whole area of territory comprised in Sonoma county is greatly influenced in climate, productions, etc., by its contiguity to the ocean, a considerable portion of it forming the boundary coast line. Dense and heavy fogs arise from the sea every morning, creating a dampness and a dew which admirably supply the place of rain, and serve at once to irrigate and fertilize the soil, preventing those parching droughts so destructive to crops, and so discouraging to agriculturists in more inland portions of the State. Consequently the harvests of such cereals and fruits as are adaptable to climate and soil are always reliable. The nights and mornings are too cool for the rapid growth required in the successful culture of corn, preventing its development and maturity, though the soil around the foot-hills is as fertile as in Illinois and the more central States of the Union.

The summer and early autumn fruits yield so abundantly, that trees break and split beneath the burden of their delicious harvests. Peaches and plums of many varieties are exceedingly plentiful, and in flavor and quality are unexcelled in any quarter of the world. Apples become wrinkled and tasteless after being gathered a short time. They are largely imported from the Southren counties of Oregon, where they grow and mature finely.

Petaluma, sixteen miles southward among the mountains, lies contiguous to a shallow stream, or, rather arm of the ocean, of sufficient depth when the tide is in, to be navigable for vessels carrying from sixty to one hundred tons burden. It is a quiet, orderly little place, with fewer whisky shops than the towns and villages in its neighborhood. Most of the early Spanish settlers have sold out and emigrated to Mexico, and other congenial localities, and a different class of people taken their places. Consequently, the cock and dog fights, which were formerly the Sunday afternoon entertainments, have become extinct, and the seventh day is quiet and respected; business in the police courts is dull, and peace and order reign in the few bar-rooms which yet remain. A fine public library and two newspapers speak well for the intelligence of this little community on the Pacific. One of its drawbacks, however, is the great scarcity of fresh water. Owing to the long drouth, the cisterns are empty, and as the water from the stream is salt, this precious element of life is brought from a distance in casks, upon drays, and sold for seventy-five cents per hogshead. The streets are sprinkled with the salt water from the stream. Grass and herbage are sere and brown, but here and there fine patches of newly planted vegetables and fields of cereals are green and fresh, being nurtured by the heavy ocean fogs and dews.

The climate is cool and invigorating, and the dampness of the fogs is not unsalubrious, its effects being the same as in England, and its people greatly resemble those of that island in color, complexion and form. An old adobe house, formerly the home of an ancient Spanish governor, is quite a curiosity. It was built anterior to the ceding of

California to the Union, and has been used as a fort in the Indian wars. Now it is a peaceable, dirty farm house; the cows are milked within its courtyard, and poultry roost upon its verandahs, while pigs are fed from troughs beneath, and their owners live within its thick mud walls, all dwelling together in peace, like the happy family of a museum.

HEALDSBURG

IS a beautifully located little town on the Russian River, in the central portion of Sonoma county. It is nestled amid the mountains, and its ocean breezes render its climate pleasant and very salubrious. It numbers about one thousand inhabitants, and is connected by a railroad with Santa Rosa, the county seat of Sonoma county. Though saline lands of a gentle nature are found now and then, their stony, glassy substances have no poisonous or destructive effects upon the poultry that feed upon them, as in other portions of the State. Small cereals yield largely, and even mature in protected localities. The water of the mountain springs is deliciously cool, soft and clear, and Mother Nature has bountifully endowed the regions in the vicinity, far and near. The character of much of the population is a serious drawback to progressive growth. It is principally composed of emigrants from Missouri and the Southwestern States, who are not particularly enlightened according to the ideas of Eastern progressionists. They make it their boast that they "don't car to read nothin' no how!" are disgusted with common schools and railroads, and "stuck-up Northerners," and speak of "selling off" and "clarin' out" to "new diggins" in some unexplored wilderness where the Yankee is not, and where they can end their conservative lives without being tormented by the progressive institution of Yankeedom. Twenty-four miles from Healdsburg are located the Geysers or wonderful California hot springs. In a tract of land embracing about one square mile, many of these springs are found, boiling and bubbling up from the bosom of mother earth, antidotes for numerous diseases and ailments which afflict her children. From some of these, pure soda may be obtained, and others are greatly impregnated with sulphur, epsom salts, copperas, salt and iron. They are becoming quite a resort, and have been visited during the past summer by tourists and invalids from the States and other portions of California. Their curative powers for rheumatism, and particularly dyspepsia, are really remarkable. Cases of the latter, of twenty years' standing, have been cured by the use of these waters in a week. There are also springs within three miles of Healdsburg, possessing excellent curative properties, but not as celebrated as the Geysers.

SANTA ROSA,

THE county seat of Sonoma county, is situated on Santa Rosa Creek, an arm of the Russian River, and is reached by rail from Petaluma, sixteen miles southward. Its population is very similar in nature and characteristics to that of Healdsburg and the surrounding country. A fine park of live oaks, directly in front of the court-house, reminds the tourist of Florida, and gives a tropical appearance to the scene, both by their inviting and luxuriant shade, and the otherwise careless and ill kept appearance of the park. The court-house, an oldfashioned building of red brick, is surmounted by a dome, ornamented with a marble statue of the Goddess of Justice, with her blinded eyes and evenly poised scales.

UPPER PART OF NEVADA COUNTY IN APRIL.

AT Bloomfield, the almond and peach trees are in blossom. Five miles north, towards Moore's Flat, the snow is so deep that a wheeled conveyance must be changed for a sleigh, and the horses "slump" knee deep at every step. "How is that for altitude?" One's eyes must be protected from the glare of the sunshine upon the snow, or he may find himself nearly blind from the effect.

There is upon the north side of these mountain trees, a beautiful moss of the most delicate green. This is an inch or two in length and appears like hair, forming an overcoat for the north side of the tree, to protect it from the snows and winds of winter.

It is a strange thing that the people in these

mining towns should keep such immense bull-dogs. Nearly every other yard is ornamented with one of these unhappy creatures, fastened to a stake. Owing to the diligence and enterprise natural to this breed of dogs, they are compelled to whine out a miserable existence of imprisonment in the open air, literally spoiling for an insurance agent or an itinerant book-peddler.

The style of this chapter reminds me of a conversation I held to-day with a small boy about the size of a bag-pudding, who was barefooted and engaged in hunting patches of snow for a sled made of a dilapidated washboard turned bottom upwards and bearing the patentee's name. I will here state that I found this boy as utterly incapable of sticking to a proposition and making a point, as some of our modern lecturers. When interrogated as to who might be the builder of his sled, he answered that "he had a shoe-string in his pocket, and that he would rather go to Uncle Abe's and get some gum."

COLFAX, CAL.

THE town of Colfax has now reached the age when, like most of its mountain contemporaries, it lives more in the past than the present or future. It is a pretty lively place about train time; after that is past, it relapses into a gentle slumber, like a family watch-dog after the occasion for excitement is over. The people here think it vain to take a man's name until he has lived his life, breathed his last, and been carried out as dead as Julius Cæsar.

I wish the United States would go to war with some foreign power, the Kingdom of the Sandwich Islands, for instance, Mexico or some of the South American States, and make George Francis Train the General. There is a class of men living in every country who are only fit for a mark to shoot and California has her share of this blear-eyed population; men whose highest aim in life is to see how much whisky or lager beer they can hold. I had an encounter with a specimen the day I left Grass Valley. This genius was bound to sit upon the seat with me, and also that I should partake of the contents of his whisky flask. To this I demurred and filed a stay of proceedings. He seemed however, to recognize the accepted fact that women only live by toleration in communities, and that they travel entirely upon the strength of man's generosity and forbearance. He gently reminded me of these facts, and when we reached Colfax, he searched to find if I had a big brother that he might thrash, while I went in search of a warrant. Alas for justice in Colfax! She has the rheumatism, and is slow as molasses in January! Before I could get the papers made out, and completed with the legal formula, the train came along and carried this American voter where the " woodbine twineth," and I was cheated of that revenge so sweet, especially to women.

A remarkable catastrophe occurred in Colfax a short time ago. Two cats were playing upon the railroad track, in front of the depot, when a train came along, ran over them, and, strange to say, cut the ears off both cats, and one had his tail taken off, while Providence, in His wisdom and mercy, spared the caudal appendage of the other. This is a fact, and the cats may be seen at any time in Colfax, alive and well.

Colfax has also its regular brindle dog, with terrible eyes and horrible teeth, grinning in a mouth that has the appearance of being lined with red flannel. O! shades of Crockett—but Crockett was never an insurance agent nor an itinerant book-peddler in a mountain town of California.

GOLD RUN.

GOLD RUN has the appearance of being a very small town. I am informed, however, that it polls as many votes as Dutch Flat, and that it sustains as many saloons. During the day, when the men are at work in the mines, the place is as quiet as a Quaker meeting; and if the Modocs we read of, were to attack this town in the day time, it would be likely to surrender until the miners returned at night with picks and empty bottles. Then it would be retaken, as the Indians would fill themselves with fire-water during the day, and it would be an easy matter to pick them off at night. and throw the bodies into the miners' flumes, where the water is so deep and runs so swiftly, that about a thousand Modocs could be disposed of in one night. Their corpses would go bobbing through, about, above, around, over and under the Sierra Nevada Mountains, and land the Lord knows where, and Providence don't care. I have fought this battle and conquered the enemy, and the people of Gold Run are entirely ignorant of the whole affair.

The hotel in this town is a good place to stop at; it is kept by a fair-haired Dane who endeavors to make the traveling public a comfortable home for the time; the yards are nicely cleaned. The grounds about these country hotels generally abound in old boots, shoes, rags, hats, bones, oyster-cans, cast-off paper collars and uncorked bottles. This mixture, in all stages of decay, sends up a thousand odors to the sleeping apartments of the wretched traveler, and if it were not that his days are spent entirely in the open air, he must surely contract the lame leg epidemic, the cerebro spinal meningitis, or perish for the want of breath.

The men of this place have called Scripture to their aid, and justify themselves in working on Sundays as well as week days, by quoting that the Sabbath was made for man, not man for the Sabbath. There has been a Bible agent here holding prayer meetings. This will do among women, for it is an acknowledged fact that the gods will never hold woman responsible for the work she performs on Sunday. This agent said something to a woman about "Her lambs that had been taken to the upper fold." He also spoke of the woman as a "dam," and of the shepherd. I waited to hear if he would mention the man's name in the figurative sense. He said nothing more, but went his way, and shortly after I met him serenely sitting in the door of a saloon—the great leveler of creeds and nationalities when it comes to business.

An acquaintance of mine gives it as his opinion that I have been afflicted with "catology from early life." He might have added "dogmatics" also. These animals form a part of our domestic institutions. I love them and sympatize with them, and recognize their right to life, liberty and the pursuit of happiness, providing the happiness of the animal does not depend upon annihilating my unfortunate itinerate fraternity.

Gold Run has its remarkable dog. This creature has taken a prejudice against milk venders. He boards at the hotel, but has contracted with a respectable sow in a neighboring yard, to furnish him with the lacteal fluid. This canine may be seen several times a day taking his chances with the younger members of the sow's family.

DUTCH FLAT.

JUST now Dutch Flat appears somewhat like a huge bouquet of fruit blossoms, with mountain shrubs for background, and this bouquet has just been nicely showered. The clerk of the weather concluded to favor us at last with a downright good rain, and everybody put on a smile of peaceful resignation; even the frogs gave a concert at six o'clock last evening. One of the most remarkable things about this town is that it has a temperance hotel. A person can get nothing to drink in this house stronger than fresh buttermilk, and it is such a fine, wholesome beverage, that if all the saloons kept it for sale, lager beer would speedily fall into disuse. When I was sneezing at the rate of sixteen times an hour, it was with difficulty that the clerk of this hotel could be prevailed upon to visit the neighboring bar and procure a glass of rum and molasses that I might have a "night cap" in order to raise a perspiration.

There are at present not less than four citizens miners in this place who have lame feet or sore toes, and go upon crutches. This scene reminds me of a picture I used to see about forty years ago in " Peter Parley's Primary Geography." The engraving represented a fussy old pedagogue with a disabled foot resting upon a chair. This wonderful cut was underlined with the following pathetic words of appeal : " Take care, boys, do not run against my sore toe; if you do I shall tell you no more stories." Some call this a "frontispiece," but to me it was a "masterpiece," and I have asked nearly a thousand questions of as many different persons, to ascertain if possible how that old schoolmaster came to have a sore toe. Could never find any one wise enough to give me any reliable information upon the subject. Since then I have looked upon sore toes as a mystery past finding out. It would be well for Brother Taylor, the founder of the " Champions of the Red Cross," or any individual of similar enterprise, to organize a secret society known as "The Order of the Great Toe." The object of this order should be to mend broken door knobs, replace shattered window panes and readjust the tumbled down doorsteps of a poor distressed brother.

BLUE CANON.

WHEN the benevolent angel who spends most of his time in naming new places passed over this town in his christening boat, he saw that it had the appearance of being draped with a thin blue veil. The shrubs and trees showing through, made it look like beautiful tracery or raised embroidery, so he concluded to call it Blue Canon, and it has been known by that name ever since. No one ever told by whom the Book of Genesis was written, and I am not going to say how I came by the above tradition. The frogs here held a monotonous dialogue last evening. One saying, "Will you give credit! will you give credit?" Another answering, in deep bass, "I will give credit, I will give credit." A third, in a voice still "basser," said, "Don't you give credit, don't you give credit." Later in the evening, about the time honest folks retire, I heard them say, "Get up, pay up, dry up." The last clause has reference to the weather, undoubtedly. This town, like its western neighbor, Alta, has a good hotel, a telegraph office, a passenger and freight depot. Here endeth the first chapter. Directly in front of the hotel are forty Chinamen at work, having been engaged all winter clearing the track of snow and other obstructions. Now the springy bank is running down in a liquid form, and would keep the track mostly covered but for these miniature laborers.

They do so much remind me of the white headed ants. When viewed in a mass, they seem so nearly of a size, the sameness of their straw hats, and the little fussy motion is very much like ants or bees at work.

These men are paid twenty-eight dollars per head a month, and board themselves. I am exercised occasionally about the Chinese question. I think it would be well for the New York *Herald* to send Livingston Stanley to plant a Chinese colony in Central Africa. This is represented by him to be a fine country, and it would be just the place for the surplus population of China. I am at a loss to know whether the English claim Africa by right of discovery, *a la* Livingston, or whether it belongs to the New York *Herald;* if it should be the latter, I suppose it will in time be settled with some race of Democrats.

A girl eleven years of age, fell into a miner's flume and was carried about five hundred yards, passing over two falls of water in the meantime, the one twelve, the other twenty feet high. She at last caught hold of a bent and crawled out without assistance, but was so stupified that she could not tell what had happened her. She has recovered from her bruises, and is now able to attend school. She is a fleshy little dump, and says she sat upright all the way on her perilous ride. Grace Greenwood recommends this method to the ladies of Washington, who desire to descend the stone steps of that city, to gather up their skirts, and slide, as being the only reliable mode of descent.

RENO, NEVADA.

AS we proceed eastward by the C. P. R. R., the mountain peaks become magnificent in their moving mantles of transparent snows; and as the mist is driven before the wind, it forms in long folds, reaching up and down the height of the peak, and suggests the idea of thinly clad ghosts flitting around these venerable piles, playing blind-man's buff, or hide-and-seek. Although it is late in the season, many of these mighty elevations still wear dresses with white groundwork, ornamented with trees and shrubs of a very doubtful green. The breath that comes from these distant hills would lead one to believe that the Polar doors had been left ajar.

At Reno the following morning the storm still continues; it has softened into a cold, disagreeable rain, and instead of the ghostly folds of white, the mountains are draped with mantles of purple mist. At this point the Truckee river begins to prove its claims to the dignified name of river; it shows its power by branching out and surrounding little tracts of land, forming islands, imitating some corporations in its headstrong way, to surround and hold all unclaimed lands on its march to lake or ocean. Reno is situated in a dry, barren section of country, everything having a bleached appearance. The sidewalks are bleached and full of holes. The Washoe zephyr, of which Mark Twain makes mention, keeps the streets with a fearfully swept appearance; these gusts of wind literally scattering the old boots and cast-off paper collars to the four winds. One of these zephyrs caught me and I came near being scattered in the same manner. The trimmings of my skirt answered to the buckets of a dip water wheel, which the wind struck with such force as to cause a revolving motion. I might have continued turning around until this time, but the current concentrated all its forces upon my hat, and it rolled just as the plate did when the dish went after the spoon. I do not think that anything but a fairy could have caught up with it, but that it lodged by a stick of timber, where it was made to leap, dive, and dance a hornpipe by the merciless zephyr.

All serene again in this part of the country. The sun is shining on the contented face of nature as if nothing had transpired different from the ordinary course of things. It seems almost mockery for old Sol now to overcome the clouds, come out and greet with smiles the smoking earth, when nearly all kinds of vegetation have been destroyed by frost, which his timely presence might have saved. The people of Reno sing the hymn that has the line in it that says, "December's as pleasant as May." For three nights the gardens were covered with all kinds of clothing; in the dim light of the cold moon they appeared like a congregation of sleeping camels or hunch back ghosts. The ever-present sage brush is the only green thing not injured by the frost. This reminds me of the terrible impatient expression of countenance upon a little boy who was coming on the cars to California. He became so tired of the everlasting monotony of sage brush, that he turned to his father and said: Papa why don't the people cut down this ugly weed?" His father answered, "Because there are no people living here my son." Well," said the boy, in an impetuous way, "they should cut it down anyway if they do not live here."

For a few days past, during the late storm, the clouds have hung around in such impenetrable blackness, that one would be led to think that this mountain range was the nursery of all the great thunder and wind storms for the whole continent.

www.ingramcontent.com/pod-product-compliance
Lightning Source LLC
Chambersburg PA
CBHW021151230426
43667CB00006B/347